Sentence Craft

A Sentence Combining Handbook

Phillip Wade

Sentence Craft

Copyright © 2013 by Phillip Wade
All rights reserved.

ISBN-10: 1499301693
ISBN-13: 978-1499301694

To Grandpa Harry who taught me how to dream

ACKNOWLEDGMENTS

My deepest gratitude goes out to all who helped inspire the book:

Mr. Juan Balderas, my 6th grade English teacher who shared my love of computers and English;

Mr. Dale Baird who in 7th grade insisted I circle my prepositional phrases to set them off from my subjects and verbs;

Mrs. Valice Lauramee, my 8th grade English teacher who, passionate about teaching personal and descriptive writing, entered my award-winning essay in a county contest, the first piece I published;

Mr. Jim James and Ms. Jill Flamm, respectively my high school honors and AP English teachers, who kindled my passion for English;

My librarian grandmother Ada Wade who always ensured I had the latest computer;

My father who led the way in teaching English;

My brother Eric who programmed the Sentence Craft random generator;

Professor Brock Dethier who kept me sailing in the straits of teaching when Sirens songs nearly led me astray;

Professor Mike Sweeney who ushered me into the world of journalism;

Those at Mojang, the designers of Minecraft;

Santeri Koivisto, Aleksi Postari, and educator Joel Levin of TeacherGaming for their creation of the Minecraft education mod Minecraft.edu, which has made the game easily accessible to classrooms across the world;

Harry Noden for his groundbreaking book *Image Grammar* that opened my mind to new ways of teaching sentence structure;

Bill Strong for the many lessons I have learned while teaching with his *Sentence Combining: A Composing Book* and for his encouraging words as one of my student teaching advisors;

Don and Jenny Killgallon for their teaching tips found in their book *Paragraphs for High School;*

My wife Jennifer and my kids who have been there all the way;

And the many others who go unnamed but not forgotten.

Table of Contents

Acknowledgements — 5

Introductory Information — 9-17
- Introduction and Skills to Emphasize — 9
- Example Sentence Crafting — 10
- Quick Reference: The Ingredients — 11-13
- Punctuation Marks — 14-15
- Punctuation Patterns — 16-17

Part I: Crafting Recipes — 18
- The Crafting Table — 19-20
- How to Craft Sentences from Recipes — 21
- How to Create Recipes — 22

Simple Sentence Crafting — 23-32
- Without Top Row Master Blocks — 25-26
- With Top Row Master Blocks — 27-30
- Crafting Practice: Simple Sentence Recipes — 31-32

Compound Sentence Crafting — 33-40
- Without Top Row Master Blocks — 35-36
- With Top Row Master Blocks — 37-38
- Crafting Practice: Compound Sentence Recipes — 39-40

Complex Sentence Crafting — 41-49
- Without Top Row Master Blocks — 42
- With Top Row Master Blocks — 45-47
- Crafting Practice: Complex Recipes — 48-49

Compound Complex Sentence Crafting — 50-56
- Without Top Row Master Blocks — 51-52
- With Top Row Master Blocks — 53-54
- Crafting Practice: Compound-Complex Recipes — 55-56

Part II: The Ingredients   57-96

Bottom Row Ingredients Section I: 58
Independent Clauses
Bottom Row Terms   59
Foundation (Independent) Clause [SV]   60-63
    Nouns for Subjects and Objects   62
    Action Verbs to Consider   63
Extended Foundation Clause [SV+]   64

Bottom Row Ingredients Section II: 65
Conjunctions
Coordinating Conjunction [,cc]   66
Conjunctive Adverb [;ca,]   67
Semi-Colon [;]   68
Conjunction Wild [cj]   69

Middle Row Ingredients   70
Middle Row Terminology   71
Subordinate Dependent Clause [SSV]   72-73
Relative Pronoun Dependent Clause [RSV]   74-75
Dependent Clause Wild [DSV]   76
Dependent Clause Series [DSVS]   77-78

Top Row Ingredients: Master Blocks   79
Master Block Wild [MB]   80
Master Block Crafting Tips   81
Prepositional Phrase [PRE]   82-83
Participial Phrase [PAR]   84-85
Appositive Phrase [APP]   86-87
Absolute Phrase [AB]   88-89
Inserted Adjective [AJ]   90-91
Inserted Adverb [AV]   92-93
Master Block Series Wild [MBS]   94-95

Tips for Teaching Sentence Craft — 96-104

    Sample Sentence Craft Unit — 97-98
    Daily Recipe Exercise Process — 99
    Other Teaching Tips — 100
    Teaching with Minecraft.edu — 101-102
    Sample Refining Options — 103-104

Appendix — 105-109

    Student Crafting Activity Sheet — 106-107
    Practice Sentence Crafting Examples — 108-109

Sources and Other Resources — 110

Introduction to Sentence Craft

Skills to Emphasize

Objective 1: Use a variety of sentence lengths and structures, including simple, compound, complex, and compound-complex.

Objective 2: Punctuate effectively within the rules and without.

Objective 3: Write concisely using specific nouns and lively action verbs.

Objective 4 Craft using master techniques (creative words and phrases) in a variety of forms: basic, extended, and series.

Objective 5: Use and understand the terminology.

Objective 6: Apply the concepts learned in Sentence Craft to standardized tests and more extended writing situations, including narrative, expository (informational), and argumentative.

Author's note

Since my first year teaching general 9th and 10th grade English in 1999, I have sought out engaging and unique ways to help my students write more effective sentences. The journey I embarked upon all those years ago eventually led me to write this book.

Early in those years, no matter how hard I tried to make sentence combining activities engaging, I was too often greeted by resistant groans. So I started experimenting with ways that I could make such activities more interesting to the average student. Those experiments led me to create activities that used video games either literally (when they wrote about or redesigned them) or as metaphors for teaching writing in engaging ways.

How does *Sentence Craft* work? Well, the journey begins with teaching or learning the blocks and methods outlined in this book.

See the next page for an example crafting recipe and a demonstration of the sentence crafting process.

Example Crafting Recipe

Where did the recipe come from?
When teaching Sentence Craft, the teacher provides the recipe. See page 22 for instructions. Recipes are also found in this book or online at sentencecraft.blogspot.com.

How does the student craft the recipe?
Instructions are found on page 21. Each block in the table represents a specific sentence part. The student may refer to the quick reference guide on pages 11-13 or the ingredients section to learn what each block represents and which row it is placed.

A recipe is read from the bottom up, one row at a time. **The bottom row** is where independent clauses and conjunctions are placed. This recipe has only one independent (foundation) clause represented by the [SV] block in the middle cell. Example crafted independent clause: *The airplane buzzed above*.

The middle row is where dependent clause blocks are placed. This recipe has a subordinate dependent clause, represented by the [SSV] block. The beginning cell means the student should attach it to the beginning of the independent (foundation) clause. Example dependent clause: *As Nathan tried to sleep*

The top row is where creative phrase or word blocks are placed. These are referred to as master blocks because they are the tools of master sentence crafters. This recipe has an appositive [APP] master block in the middle cell, meaning it should be placed in the middle of one of the clauses. Example crafted appositive identifying airplane: *a Cessna 172*

Once a student understands the recipe and its parts, he or she crafts a combined sentence. **Example crafted sentence:** *As Nathan tried to sleep, the airplane, a Cessna 172, buzzed above*.

So what is *Sentence Craft*? Is it a metaphor for understanding sentence structure and punctuation? Is it a sentence combining teaching tool? Is it a game? The answer? All of the above.

I hope *Sentence Craft* helps you as a teacher or student as much as it has helped my students and me. Enjoy the journey.

Bottom Row Blocks: Quick Reference

Foundation Blocks: Independent Clauses

Independent Foundation Clause (Wild)
The foundation of all sentences. Four patterns:

1. **Subject + Verb:** The cannon roared.
2. **Subject + Verb + Direct Object:** The swashbucklers drew swords.
3. **Subject + Verb + Prepositional Phrase:** Bullets sliced through the air.
4. **Subject + Linking Verb + Complement:** The ship is a frigate.

Extended Independent Foundation Clause
Represents an independent clause with a compound element / series (subject, verb, object, complement)

1. Subject series: *The zombie and the mob* hunted Steve in the brewing darkness.
2. Verb series: The creeper *hissed, screeched, trembled* as it died in the sun.
3. Direct object series: Steve damaged his *shoulder, knee,* and *ankle* in the fall.
4. Prepositional phrase series: Steve dug *through gravel, past stone,* and *into the dark*.
5. Complement series: The passage appears *dark, steep,* and *slippery*.

Compounding Conjunctions

Coordinating Conjunction: *and, but, or, nor, for, so, yet*
The most common form of compounding conjunction, a coordinating conjunction joins two independent clauses into a compound sentence. Precede with a comma unless either clause is four words or less.

Zombies moaned in the distance, *so* Steve retreated to his hovel.

Conjunctive Adverb: *however, therefore, thus, nevertheless, then, next.*
Joins two independent clauses. The conjunctive adverb is preceded by a semi-colon and followed by a comma.

Steve needs weapons; *thus,* he smelts iron.

Semi-colon
The only punctuation mark with the power to join two independent foundation clauses on its own.

The war is over; my computer crashed.

Compounding Conjunction Wild
Represents any compounding conjunction: Sentence crafter chooses which to use.

Middle Row Blocks: Quick Reference

Dependent Clause Blocks

Subordinate Dependent Clause

Begin with Subordinating Conjunctions: *after, although, as, because, before, if, since, though, unless, until, when, whenever, while*

Example Complex Sentence Crafting:
1. **Start with a foundation clause:**
Creepers can explode.
2. **Add a subordinate conjunction to form a dependent clause:**
<u>Because</u> creepers can explode
3. **Add a new foundation clause to form a complex sentence:**
Because Creepers can explode, you should avoid them.

Relative Pronoun Dependent Clause

Begin with Relative Pronouns: *who, whom, whose, which, that*

Example Complex Sentence Crafting With Relative Pronoun Clause:
Foundation clause: Spiderman dangled from the bridge.
Subordinate Dependent clause: <u>who</u> reveled in danger.
Complex sentence: Spiderman, *who ignored the danger,* dangled from the bridge.

Dependent Clause Wild
Represents either dependent clause:
Sentence crafter chooses which to use.

 OR

Dependent Clause Series Wild
Represents either dependent clause in series.
This powerful block calls for the sentence crafter to write a series of either dependent clause type at the location requested by the recipe.

Complex Sentence with [SSV] Beginning Series
After the storm abated, before the sky had cleared, the dam broke.

Complex Sentence with [RSV] Splitting Series
The mysterious woman *who left the package on the couch, who hurried out the exit* is the prime suspect. (Essential clauses that specifically identify which woman so no bracketing commas).

Complex Sentence with [SSV] Ending Series
With repetition (Use comma): The water raged down the canyon *after the sudden storm, after the dam had broken.*
No repetition, no comma: The chandelier fell *when the crow jumped on it because Scotty chased him.*

Top Row Blocks: Quick Reference
Master Blocks

 Prepositional Phrase
   preposition + (any adjectives) + noun
1. **Basic:** above the tree, beneath the water, on the bridge, in style, with vigor
2. **Extended:** above the massive oak tree, beneath the raging water of the river
3. **Sentence:** With a roar, the Minotaur pursued Theseus *through the maze.*

 "ing" Participial Phase
   A verb + ing forming an adjective.
1. **Basic:** Hiding, dodging, delving, eluding, eroding, exploding, slipping
2. **Extended/Phrase (most common):** descending into chaos, crafting an axe
3. **Sentence:** *Following a trail of thread*, Theseus, *avoiding certain death*, escaped the maze.

 Appositive
   A noun further identifying another noun
1. **Basic (describing person):** a pediatrician, my friend, a patriot, a traitor
2. **Extended:** a successful pediatrician, my Jewish friend, a zealous patriot
3. **Sentence:** Joshua, *my Jewish friend*, admires Thomas Paine, *a zealous patriot.*

 Absolute
   noun + participle or other adjective
1. **Basic:** lungs burning, clouds brewing, legs tired, heart heavy
2. **Extended:** my lungs burning with exhaustion, clouds brewing dangerously
3. **Sentence:** *Branches clashing*, the aspen swayed in the breeze, *its trunk creaking.*

 Inserted Adjective
   Modifies a noun. Inserted into an unusual spot
1. **Basic:** harsh, soft, orange, scruffy, wooly, itchy, smooth, tarnished.
   Includes non-ing participles: tarnished, scathed, purified, worn, torn
2. **Extended:** tarnished with time, scathed badly, purified by filters, worn raw
3. **Sentence:** The frigates, *mysterious in origin*, emerged, *swift and dangerous.*

 Inserted Adverb
   Modifies a verb, adverb, or adjective. Inserted in an unusual spot. Use conjunctive adverbs for the splitting option.
1. **Basic:** cautiously, passionately, swiftly, today, tomorrow, later, soon
   includes conjunctive adverbs: *however, therefore, thus, then, nevertheless*
2. **Extended (+ adjective/participle):** effectively winning, cautiously optimistic
3. **Sentence:** *Thus*, the ninja scaled the wall, *skillfully.*

 Master Block Wild
   When this appears, the sentence crafter chooses any master block.

 Master Block Series Wild
   When this appears, the sentence crafter chooses any master block and writes it in a series of two or three.

13

Punctuation Marks

External Marks

External marks are placed between independent clauses (simple sentences).

. **Period:** The most important mark in punctuation. The period tells the reader where a sentence ends, though they are sometimes used at the end of fragments for creative effect. Knowing where to place periods is the most important punctuation skill for a writer to master. Nothing can lose your reader more than incorrectly placed or missing periods. The period can be substituted for the semi-colon, which is much less common and has a different function.

; **Semi-colon:** Interchangeable with a period, the semi-colon is used on the boundary between two related independent foundation clauses. Unlike a period, the semi-colon joins two independent clauses instead of separating them, creating a shorter pause for the reader. The semi-colon can also be used to separate sub-categories of items in a multi-category series. The semi-colon should be used sparingly. Do not confuse the semi-colon with a colon. A semi-colon is <u>not</u> used to introduce a series of items.

Advanced / Internal Marks
Internal marks are placed on the boundaries between words, phrases, and clauses that exist inside of sentences.

, **Comma:** Commas tell the reader where to pause or slow down. The main function of the comma is to indicate pauses and make the writing more clear. Commas are placed on the boundaries between words, phrases, and clauses that exist inside of sentences. Commas can be used alone or in bracketing pairs. Commas can be replaced by dashes, if you want something stronger; by parenthesis, if you want something softer. Commas should not be placed where a period or semi-colon should go.

— **Dash:** Dashes set off information from a sentence that a reader should not skip. Dashes are powerful, flexible punctuation marks that can replace colons, parenthesis, and commas. Compared with parentheses, dashes draw attention to themselves and the essential information they set aside. Dashes can be used alone or—when in the middle of a sentence—in pairs. Dashes should be used sparingly. In most cases, a comma, or pair of commas, is more appropriate. Do not confuse the dash—which is made by typing the hyphen key twice—with the hyphen, which is just one stroke of the key (-). A hyphen has different functions not relevant to Sentence Craft.

( ) **Parenthesis:** Information enclosed in parenthesis is considered unnecessary and can be skipped if the reader so chooses. Parenthesis separate more softly than commas or dashes. Parenthesis are always used in pairs and should be avoided (especially in formal papers). Typically, commas work better.

: **Colon:** The colon clues the reader that something is coming: a series, a definition, or an explanatory statement. Like a dash, a colon creates a pause, but is more formal than a dash. It typically follows a complete independent clause and is then followed by a restatement or series/list. Colons do <u>not</u> follow be verbs: *is, am, are, was, were, be, been, being.*

Sentence Craft Punctuation Patterns

Simple Sentence Patterns: One Foundation Clause

1. $\boxed{SV}$. May include multiple essential words or phrases but just one clause.
2. $\boxed{SV}$: A, B, and C.   A, B, and C represent words in a series (list).

Other series options:

   2B. A, B, C.   2C. A and B and C.   2D. A1, A2; B1, B2; and C1, C2.

Notes for Patterns 2-2D:
Pattern 2 is the standard: a colon following an independent clause.
Do not use a colon before a series that immediately follows a "be" verb.
"Be" verbs include *is, am, are, was, were, be, been, being.*
Using a comma and a conjunction before the final word in series is standard.
Patterns 2B and 2C are informal, creative series patterns.
Do not confuse a colon (:) with a semi-colon (;).
Colons introduce lists or warn that a restatement is coming.
Semi-colons join two independent clauses or separate categorie lists as in 2D.
In Pattern 2, use a dash for a stronger effect than a colon.

Simple Sentence With Top Row Master Blocks

3. $\boxed{MB}$, $\boxed{SV}$.
4. $\boxed{S}$, $\boxed{MB}$, $\boxed{V}$.
5. $\boxed{SV}$, $\boxed{MB}$.

Notes for Patterns 3-5:

MB = Master Block = Words and phrases used effectively by master writers.
[MB]=preposition, participle, appositive, adjective, or adverb used creatively.

Essential vs. Non-essential
If an added master block is essential, do not use punctuation. Use Pattern 1.
nonessential: a word or phrase not necessary to sentence. Use punctuation.
essential: If left out, the sentence lacks vital information. No punctuation.

Other Punctuation Options:
Use dashes instead of commas--to interrupt abruptly.
Use parentheses instead of commas (to blend softly).

Compound Sentence: Two Foundation Clauses

6. [SV], cc [SV].

cc = coordinating conjuction = FANBOYS = *for, and, nor, but, or, yet, so*
No comma if either side of conjunction is not independent. Use Pattern 1.

7. [SV]; ca, [SV].

ca = conjunctive adverb = *however, therefore, thus, nevertheless, consequently, then, next, moreover,* (etc.)

For a clause beginning with a conjunctive adverb, use Pattern 3.
For a conjunctive adverb inside a clause use Pattern 4.

8. [SV]; [SV].

Complex Sentence
Foundation Clause + Dependent Clause(s)

9. [DSV], [SV].

10. [S], [DSV], [V].

11. [SV][DSV].

Notes for Patterns 9-11:

DSV means dependent clause.
A **[DSV]** starts with a subordinating conjunction or relative pronoun.
  subordinating conjuctions (begin SSV clauses)= *if, after, although, as, because, before, since, though, unless, until, when, whenever, whereas*

  relative pronouns (begin RSV clauses) = *which, while, that, which, who, whoever, whom.* Note: Relative pronoun acts as subject of clause.

The same essential vs. nonessential rules apply as with patterns 3-5.
Do not use commas with essential relative pronouns.
Tips:
  Which clauses are typically non-essential. Use commas.
  That clauses are typically essential. Do not use commas.

Part I

Recipes and Sentence Craft

The Crafting Table

In the Minecraft video game, the player collects raw ingredients and places them in certain combinations and patterns on a wooden crafting table to create countless items, from critical survival equipment to luxuries such as bookcases.

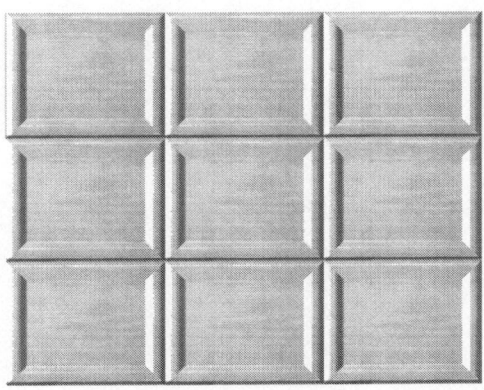

The crafting table, when selected, is actually no more than a 3 x 3 grid similar to the table on this page.

In Minecraft, to create an iron pickaxe, for example, a player drags and drops one stick icon from his/her inventory into the bottom row middle cell and another in the middle row middle cell to form the handle. The gamer then drags three iron ingots into the top three cells of the top row to form the pickaxe head. The newly constructed pickaxe now appears on the screen next to the crafting table, and the player adds the new tool to his/her inventory.

How do players learn what combinations to use for specific items? They follow crafting recipes. If you haven't played the game before, do a search on the Internet for Minecraft crafting recipes and prepare to be impressed at the variety.

Sentence Craft also uses crafting recipes, but instead of creating items, the crafter follows recipes in this book (or created by teachers or peers) to make creative sentences using words, phrases, and clauses as ingredients.

Sentence Craft

The Main Crafting Table Key

Master Block Beginning	Master Block Splitting	Master Block Ending
Dependent Clause Beginning	Dependent Clause Splitting	Dependent Clause Ending
Beginning Foundation Clause (Compound)	Foundation Clause (Simple) / Conjunction (Compound)	Ending Foundation Clause (Compound)

The above is called the **main crafting table key**. Here, the specific use for each cell is labeled to guide recipe crafters in placing blocks and sentence crafters in writing sentences based on those recipes. It may look a little confusing at first, and that's okay. The rest of this handbook is dedicated to teaching you how to use this table, one sentence type at a time. When you are crafting recipes or sentences, you can refer to this page—and to the other keys in the pages that follow—at any time for a reminder of what each cell represents.

The next two pages outline how to follow recipes to craft sentences and then how to create your own recipes.

After those two explanatory pages, the next pages will take you step-by-step through sentence crafting, beginning with simple sentences and then leading into compound, complex, and, finally, compound-complex.

Let's get started.

The Crafting Table
How to Follow Recipes

1. Determine Sentence Type Using Bottom Two Rows
Simple Sentence: Only *one* independent clause block in the foundation (bottom) row and *no* blocks in the middle row.
Compound Sentence: Two independent clauses in the foundation row with a conjunction in the middle.
Complex Sentence: One independent clause in the foundation row and one or more dependent clauses in the middle row.
Compound-Complex: Two independent clauses and a conjunction in foundation row with at least one dependent clause in the middle row.

2. Craft the Clauses
Simple Sentence (Foundation Row)
Craft the independent foundation clause.
Compound Sentence (Foundation Row)
-Craft the first (left column) independent foundation clause.
-Craft the conjunction and punctuate following patterns 6-8.
-Craft the second (right column) independent foundation clause.
Complex Sentence (Foundation and Middle Rows)
-Craft the independent foundation clause first.
-Add middle row dependent clause(s) to the independent clause and/or any other dependent clause(s) in the beginning (left column), splitting (middle column), or ending position (right column). Use patterns 9-11.
Compound Complex (Foundation and Middle Rows)
-Craft the two independent foundation clauses.
-Add the requested conjunction, following patterns 6-8.
-Add dependent clause(s) to either or both independent clauses.
-Place each dependent clause in the position the recipe calls for (beginning, splitting, or ending) for whichever independent foundation clause you have chosen to connect it to. Punctuate the dependent clause boundaries using patterns 9-11.

3. Add Top Row Master Blocks if in Recipe
-Add master block(s) to the clause(s) in the sentence.
-Left cell means the beginning of *any* clause, even if dependent.
-Middle cell means between subject and verb of *any* clause.
-End cell means end of *any* clause. Punctuate: patterns 3-5.

Sentence Craft

How to Create Recipes
(Typically, the recipe crafter is the teacher)

-When creating recipes for inexperienced sentence crafters, use keystone blocks only: [SV], [,cc], [SSV], [PAR], [PRE], [APP]

-Typically, you should use no more than two dependent clause blocks in the middle row of the table. Doing so keeps sentences more natural—especially with complex sentences which may have various dependent clauses and master blocks to connect to only one independent clause.

-If time is limited, I recommend including no more than one block in the middle row and no more than one in the top row for compound/complex recipes using all three rows of the table.

-Don't expect perfection, especially with beginning crafters. Although sentence crafters should strive to follow each recipe, and to learn the differences between the blocks, they should be free to expand upon the sentence, extending its various elements, adding additional clauses and phrases as desired. After all, the central goal is to help apprentice crafters write longer, more complex sentences.

-Use the space above the table either to write a suggested topic or a basic independent foundation clause for sentence crafters to start with. Encourage crafters to approach provided topics or sentences uniquely, anticipating what less original sentence crafters might write and then creatively doing otherwise. Although you will often keep your topics fairly general in nature to provide flexibility, remind sentence crafters to choose specific nouns and action verbs.

-Be creative with the refine option. This option enables you as a recipe crafter to add specific instructions beneath the table. Be creative with the things you ask the crafters of your recipe to do. See pages 103-104 in the "Tips for Teaching Sentence Craft" section for specific refining tips.

The Crafting Table

Simple Sentence Crafting

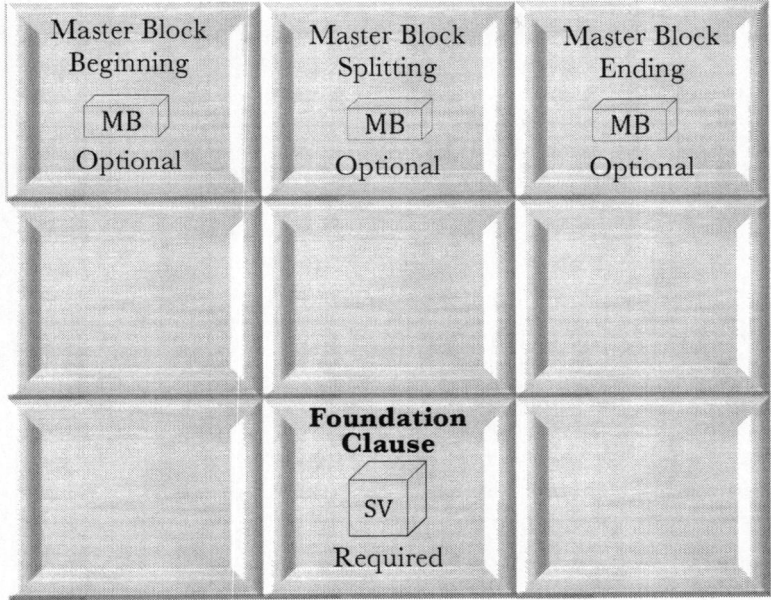

Above is the **simple sentence crafting table recipe key**. A simple sentence includes only one foundation clause (see page 60 for details), and it may include additional words and phrases as well. When crafting simple sentences, only the four cells labeled above are used.

The bottom middle cell is where a foundation clause block is placed and required. There are really only two options: an independent clause foundation block [SV] (see pg. 60) or an extended foundation clause with an element series [SV+] (see page 64). Both represent basic simple sentence forms.

The top three cells are where master blocks [MB] may be optionally placed (see page 80). Master blocks are the spice that professional writers add to their sentences, the techniques that separate master sentence crafters from apprentices. Follow punctuation patterns 3-5 when inserting master blocks.

Sentence Craft

Example Simple Sentences

Three Simple Sentence Forms
Simple sentences include only one independent foundation clause, but may include any number of additional words and phrases.

1. Independent (Foundation) Clause [SV]
A basic simple sentence follows any independent clause pattern:

S +V: Jonathan awoke.

S + V + DO: The snow blanketed the desert.

S + V + PR: The mountains collapsed into the sea.

S + LV + C: The stranger seems nice.

2. Independent Clause Extended [SV+]
This form of simple sentence follows the [SV+] block patterns. Here are the same sentences above but with additional (compound) elements: subjects, verbs, direct objects, prepositional phrases, or complements.

Subjects: *Jonathan* and *Breanna* awoke.

Verbs: Jonathan *awoke, stretched, yawned*.

Direct Objects: The snow blanketed *the desert, the Bedouin camp,* and *the surrounding hills*.

Prepositional phrases: The mountain collapsed *onto the shore* and *into the sea*.

Complements: The stranger seems *nice* but *distant*.

3. Independent Clause Plus Master Blocks (Added Creative Words or Phrases)
Moaning softly, Jonathan, *my son,* awoke. [PAR], [APP]

Surprising the nomads, the snow blanketed the desert and the Bedouin camp, *falling from a cloudy sky*. [SV+] + [PAR]

Slopes crumbling, the mountains collapsed into the sea, *sending plumes of dust across the island*. [AB], [PAR]

The stranger, *a mysterious Swede,* seems nice but distant.

[SV+] +[AB]

Simple Sentence Crafting

Example Recipe 1: Simple Sentence, No Master Blocks

Well here it is, the moment you've been waiting for—your first recipe. Above is the most simple recipe in Sentence Craft.

Following the Recipe

Even though there is only one block, the definition page for the [SV] block on page 60 of the ingredients section of this handbook explains that this block actually represents four possible patterns. The crafter may choose from any of the four, though patterns 2 and 3 are recommended. For the sake of example, I'll craft one of all four.

Example Crafted Sentences (Four Variations):

1. Subject + verb

   The rose bloomed.

2. Subject + Verb + Direct Object

   Sir Lancelot sought the Holy Grail.

3. Subject + Verb + Prepositional Phrase

   Sir Galahad disappeared into the forest.

4. Subject + linking verb + complement.

   Sir Galahad was the son of Lancelot.

Sentence Craft

Example Recipe 2: Simple Sentence, No Master Blocks

Following the Recipe (See page 21.)

This recipe calls for the [SV+] extended foundation clause block. Review this block and the provided examples in the bottom row section of the ingredients. I will craft three example sentences, all with one clause having an element series. Use series punctuation pattern 2, 2B, or 2C.

Series of two subjects:
Jefferson and *Madison* altered the world forever.

Series of three verbs:
The Liberty Bell tolled, vibrated, cracked *on Washington's birthday in 1846.* (Note: Lack of conjunction is non-standard / informal.)

Series of three direct objects:
The bullet penetrated the target sheet, *a* Wheaties box, *and the* Jacobsen's fence.

Variation: Series of three verbs combined with prepositional phrases with no conjunction:
News of Kennedy's assassination swept *across the continent,* travelled *over the sea, and* spread *through the remotest parts of the globe.*

Simple Sentence Crafting

Master Block Form Options

A **master block** is a word or phrase added creatively to a sentence. The use of master blocks is what separates master writers from amateurs. Typically, a master block has three options that the sentence crafter may use when a block appears in a recipe: **basic, extended,** and **series**. If desired, a recipe writer can provide instructions requesting a particular option in the refine field at the bottom of the crafting table. The recipe writer might, for example, request that master blocks take the extended form. Otherwise, the sentence crafter chooses which form to use.

Basic: The basic option is a master block's most simple form.

Extended: Master blocks can be extended by adding additional modifying words. A prepositional phrase, for example, can be extended by adding additional adjectives. Thus, the basic prepositional phrase *on the sea* could be extended to *on the deep blue sea*.

Series: A series is a list. Crafters can make lists of either basic or extended master block forms. Master block series forms are typically two or three elements long. Crafting in series adds rhythm to sentences and can be done in all forms of writing.

Series Options (With Participle Examples)

Standard: commas with conjunction before end
*Blinking, glowing, **and** steaming,* the lights melted the snow.

Commas only (Non-standard / Informal)
The snow, *sinking, obscuring, drifting,* blanketed the tundra.

Conjunctions only (Non-standard with three parts)
The eagle, *soaring **and** screeching,* dove for the kill.

The croc inhaled his prey, *slurping **and** gurgling **and** gagging*.

Dashes to Set off Series
Opening: *Raging through the forest, jumping over rivers, and destroying all in its path*—the fire decimated Yellowstone.

Splitting: The snowmobiler—*speeding over hillsides* and *buzzing through the darkness*—traveled home.

Ending: The volcano erupted—*spewing lava, belching fire*.

Example Recipe 3: Simple Sentence, Opening MB

Crafting the Recipe

1. **Foundation Row:** Always start with the foundation row. This recipe calls for a standard independent clause [SV].

   Foundation clause: *Waves crashed into the shore.*

2. **Top Row Master Block:** The top row shows a prepositional phrase master block in the beginning cell representing the beginning of the sentence.

   Prepositional phrase: *along Waikiki beach*

3. Combine the clause with the prepositional phrase at the beginning. Use Punctuation Pattern 3.

Crafted Simple Sentence

Along Waikiki beach, waves crashed into the shore.

Variations

Extended: *Along beautiful Waikiki beach in Honolulu,* waves crashed into the shore.

Series: *From isles unknown, across vast expanses of the Pacific, along Waikiki beach,* waves crashed into the shore.

Simple Sentence Crafting

Example Recipe 4: Simple Sentence, Splitting MB

Crafting the Recipe

1. **Foundation Row:** Always start with the foundation row. This recipe calls for a standard independent / foundation clause [SV].

    Foundation clause: *Mommy kissed Santa Clause.*

2. **Top Row Master Block:** The top row shows a participle master block in the splitting cell, meaning it should be placed between the subject and verb of the foundation clause. Like all master blocks, the [PAR] block has three options: a single word, an extended phrase, or a series. I will choose a participial phrase as that is the most common use of the participle block. Use Punctuation Pattern 4.

    Participial phrase: <u>standing</u> *beneath the mistletoe.*

3. Combine the foundation clause with the participial phrase.

Crafted Simple Sentence

*Mommy, **standing beneath the mistletoe**, kissed Santa Clause.*

Sentence Craft

Example Recipe 5: Simple Sentence, Ending MB

Crafting the Recipe

1. **Foundation Row:** Always start with the foundation row. This recipe calls for an extended independent foundation clause [SV+]. I will craft a series of three verbs for this example, although I could have crafted a series of subjects or direct objects instead. Use punctuation pattern 2, 2b, or 2B.

   Foundation clause with element series (verbs)

   The falcon soared, dove, and swooped through the canyon.

2. **Top Row Master Block:** The top row shows an appositive master block [APP] in the ending cell, meaning it should be placed at the end of the sentence. As *canyon* ends the foundation clause, I will craft an appositive that modifies that noun.

   Appositive phrase: *an isolated part of Yellowstone*.

3. Combine the clause with the appositive phrase.

Crafted Simple Sentence

The falcon soared, dove, and swooped through the canyon, ***an isolated part of Yellowstone***.

Simple Sentence Crafting

Simple Sentence Keystones Practice

Refer to page 21 for instructions.

1. Topic: Soccer

Practice Sentence:

Your Sentence:

Refine: [PRE] series

2. Topic: A race

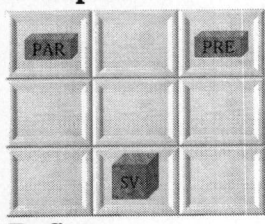

Practice Sentence:

Your Sentence:

Refine:

3. Topic: A diver

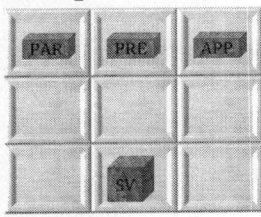

Practice Sentence:

Your Sentence:

Refine:

See pg. 108 for example sentences.

Sentence Craft
Simple Sentence Advanced Practice
Refer to page 21 for instructions.

4. Topic: A windmill

Practice Sentence:

Your Sentence:

Refine: None

5. Topic: A speaker

Practice Sentence:

Your Sentence:

Refine: None

6. Topic: A spacecraft

Practice Sentence:

Your Sentence:

Refine:
Use a conjunctive adverb.

See pg. 109 for example sentences.

Compound Sentence Crafting

Compound Sentence Crafting

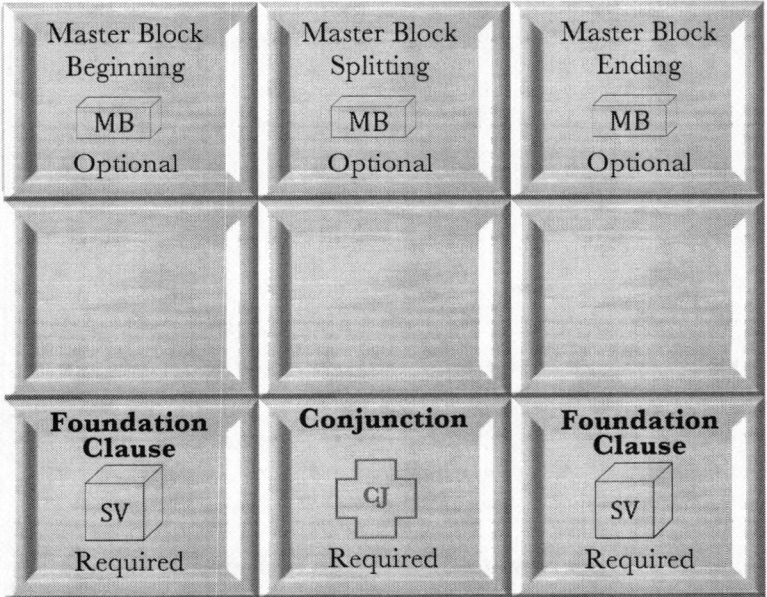

When a crafter joins two foundation clauses to build one sentence, it is referred to as a **compound sentence**. Thus, the recipe for a compound sentence means placing two foundation clause blocks on the bottom row as shown in the above pattern key.

The beginning cell in the row of the key represents the first foundation clause in the sentence (represented by the keystone SV) while the ending cell represents the second clause. The **conjunction** that joins the two clauses is placed in the middle cell, represented in this case by the [CJ] wild block. Use punctuation patterns 6-8 for adding conjunctions.

Master blocks represented by the [MB] can be added to the top row, and when such is the case, the sentence crafter decides which clause to incorporate the master block(s), placing the blocks in the beginning, splitting, or ending positions of either clause. Use punctuation patterns 3-5.

Sentence Craft

Example Compound Sentences

The same two independent foundation clauses can be combined into a compound sentence in any of three ways:
1. With a comma and coordinating conjunction
2. With a conjunctive adverb preceded by a semi-colon and followed by a comma
3. With a semi-colon.

Below is an example of the same two foundation clauses being combined to form compound sentences in these three different ways.

Same Independent Foundation Clauses, Different Conjunctions
The sands covered the ruins, **and** *time erased the cobbled streets.*
The sands covered the ruins; **thus,** *time erased the cobbled streets.*
The sands covered the ruins; time erased the cobbled streets.

Note: Do not confuse an extended independent foundation clause [SV+] with a compound sentence.
Although an [SV+] may have more than one subject and/or verb, and may include a conjunction, it is still just one clause and, thus, is not a compound sentence.

Example [SV+]:
Hurricane Katrina decimated the coast and caused millions of dollars in damage.

The above sentence has a compound verb (*decimated* and *caused*) joined by a conjunction but still has only one [SV+] foundation clause. Therefore, it is a simple sentence, not a compound one.

Also remember that a complete foundation clause must follow the coordinating conjunction to form a compound sentence. In the above case, *caused millions of dollars* is not a clause because it lacks a subject. Thus, no comma is placed before the conjunction *and*.

Compound Sentence Crafting

Example Recipe 5: Standard Compound Sentence

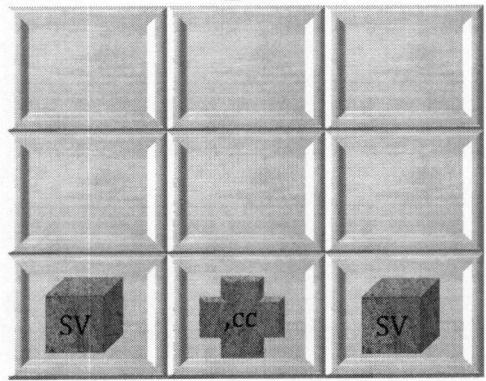

Crafting the Recipe

1. **Foundation Row: Two Independent Clauses**

   a. Standard foundation clause [SV] in the beginning:
   The tornado missed Norman, Oklahoma.

   b. Standard foundation clause [SV] in end:
   It touched down in Oklahoma City.

   c. Coordinating conjunction block [,cc].
   Choose a FANBOY: *for, and, nor, but, or, yet, so.*
   With the above two clauses, *but* will work best.

   d. Use Punctuation Pattern 6.

Crafted compound sentence

The tornado missed Norman, Oklahoma, but it touched down in Oklahoma City.

Variations With Different Conjunction Blocks:

With [;ca,] block: *The tornado missed Norman, Oklahoma; however, it touched down in Oklahoma City.*

With [;] block: *The tornado missed Norman, Oklahoma; it touched down in Oklahoma City.*

Example Recipe 6: Compound Sentence

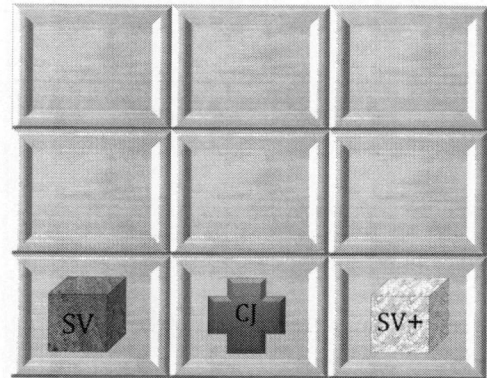

Crafting the Recipe

1. **Foundation Row: Two Independent Clauses**

    a. Standard independent clause [SV] in the beginning:

    The wolf howled in the distance.

    b. Extended independent clause [SV+] in end. I will craft a clause with two subjects:

    My <u>poodle</u> and my <u>kitten</u> huddled together.

    c. The [CJ] wild means I can choose any of the three conjunction patterns [,cc], [;ca,] or [;].

    d. Use Punctuation Pattern 7.

    Crafted compound sentence with [,cc]

    The wolf howled in the distance, so my poodle and kitten huddled together.

    Crafted compound sentence with [;ca,]

    The wolf howled in the distance; therefore, my poodle and kitten huddled together.

    Crafted compound sentence with [;]

    The wolf howled in the distance; my poodle and kitten huddled together.

Compound Sentence Crafting

Example Recipe 7: Compound With Master Block

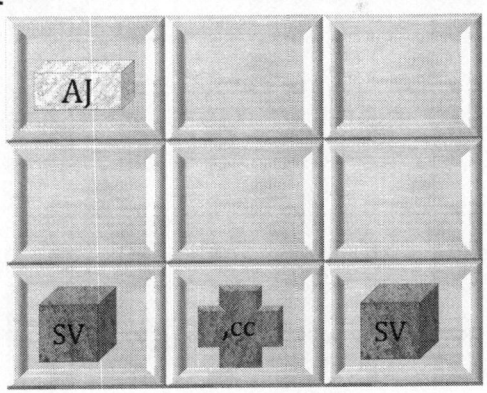

Crafting the Recipe

1. **Foundation Row: Two Independent Clauses**

    a. Standard independent clause [SV] in the beginning:
    The tide effaced the footprints.

    b. Standard independent clause [SV] in the end:
    The moon watched from above.

    c. Coordinating conjunction with comma (Pattern 7): , *and*

2. **Top Row Master Block**

    a. The top row shows an inserted adjective master block [AJ]. It is in the beginning cell, meaning at the beginning of one of the clauses. As adjectives are often inserted in series, we will use the series option here. **Adjectives:** *luminous, curious, alone.* Punctuation Patterns 2b series and 3.

    b. With compound sentences, the crafter chooses which foundation clause receives the master block(s). I'll place the opening inserted adjective series before the second clause.

Crafted Compound Sentence: *The tide effaced the footprints,* and ***curious, luminous, alone**, the moon watched from above.*

Sentence Craft

Example Recipe 8: Compound With Three Master Blocks

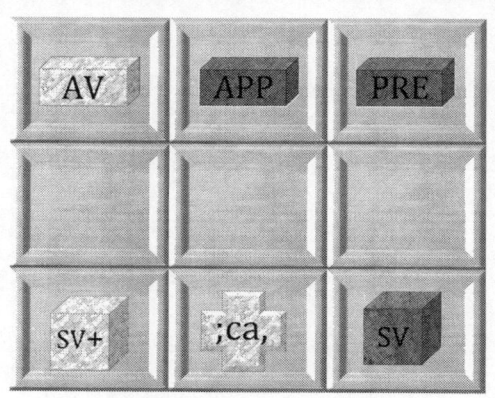

Crafting the Recipe

1. **Foundation Row: Two Independent Clauses**

    a. Extended independent clause [SV+] in the beginning:
    <u>Squids</u> and <u>sharks</u> infest this troubled sea.   Pattern 2c

    b. Standard independent clause [SV] in the end:
    We need to stay in the skiff.

    c. Conjunctive adverb: *therefore*   Punctuation Pattern 7

2. **Top Row Master Blocks**

    a. Beginning inserted adverb [AV]: *unfortunately*

    b. Splitting appositive phrase [APP]: *ravenous <u>predators</u>*

    c. Ending participle [PAR]. I'll craft a series of phrases: *<u>avoiding</u> the reefs, <u>hoping</u> the sun will rise.*

    d. Crafter chooses which foundation clause receives each master block. I'll place [AV] and [APP] in the first and the [PRE] in the second.

    e. Use punctuation patterns 3-5 for master blocks.

Crafted Compound Sentence: *Unfortunately, squids and sharks, **ravenous predators**, infest this troubled sea; therefore, we need to stay in the skiff, **avoiding the reefs, hoping the sun will rise**.*

Compound Sentence Crafting

Compound Sentence Keystones Practice
Refer to page 21 for instructions.

1. Foundation Clause: The raft approached the rapid.

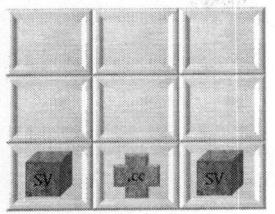

Practice Sentence:

Your Sentence:

Refine:

2. Topic: A bird

Practice Sentence:

Your Sentence:

Refine: Use a series of prepositional phrases.

3. Topic: A bungee jumper

Practice Sentence:

Your Sentence:

Refine: Do not use *and* as the [,cc].

See pg. 108 for example sentences.

Sentence Craft
Compound Sentence Advanced Practice
Refer to page 21 for instructions.

4. Topic: A caterpillar

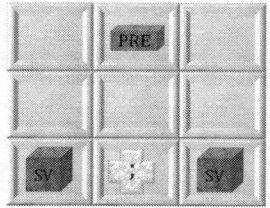

Practice Sentence:

[PRE] [SV ; SV]

Your Sentence:

Refine:

5. Topic: Outlaws

Practice Sentence:

[APP] [AJ] [SV+ ;ca, SV]

Your Sentence:

Refine:
Use a series of inserted adjectives.

6. Topic: A tree

Practice Sentence:

[AV] [AB] [PAR] [SV CJ SV]

Your Sentence:

Refine: Use a dash.

See pg. 109 for example sentences.

Complex Sentence Crafting

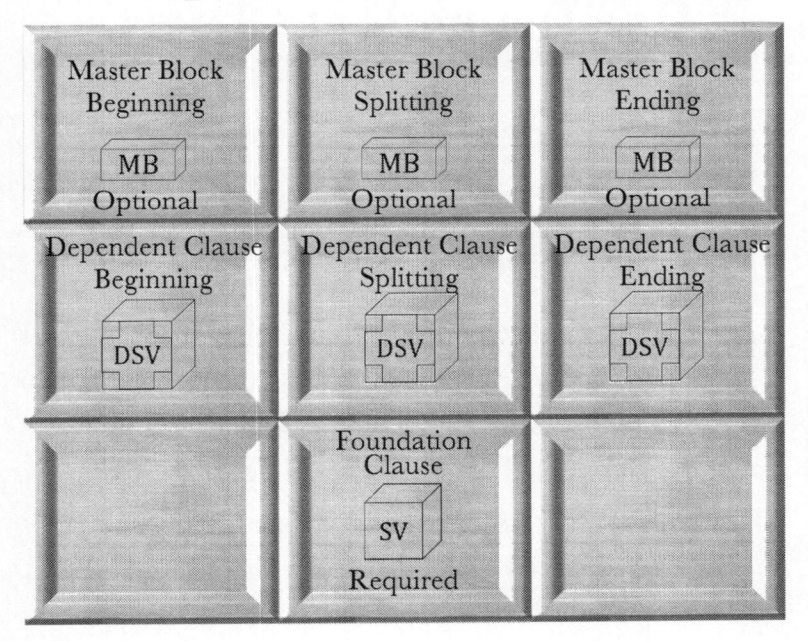

Master Block Beginning [MB] Optional	Master Block Splitting [MB] Optional	Master Block Ending [MB] Optional
Dependent Clause Beginning [DSV]	Dependent Clause Splitting [DSV]	Dependent Clause Ending [DSV]
	Foundation Clause [SV] Required	

Foundation Row: The bottom row of the complex sentence table functions that same as with the simple sentence table.

Middle Row: To form a complex sentence, at least one dependent clause block, represented above by the [DSV] wild block, must be placed in one of the cells of the middle row. The beginning cell represents adding a dependent clause to the beginning, the splitting cell represents a dependent clause splitting between the subject and verb of the foundation clause, and the ending cell represents adding a dependent clause to the end. Follow punctuation patterns 9-11 for complex sentences.

Top Row: Like with all sentence types, master blocks may be included but are optional. Master blocks may be placed in <u>any</u> clause (including dependent) in the requested position. For example, a beginning participle may be placed at the beginning of the last clause.

Example Recipe 9: Complex One Dependent Clause

Crafting the Recipe

1. **Foundation Row Independent Clause**

   Boulders tumbled down the mountainside.

2. **Middle Row Dependent Clause**

   a. [SSV] means a clause beginning with a subordinate conjunction: *when the Cyclops shouted*

   b. First cell of middle row means the dependent clause is placed at the beginning of the foundation clause.

   c. Use Punctuation Pattern 9.

Crafted Complex Sentence

***When the Cyclops shouted**, boulders tumbled down the mountainside.*

Variations

If the dependent clause were in the splitting cell: *Boulders, **when the Cyclops shouted**, tumbled down the mountainside.*

If the dependent clause were in ending cell: *Boulders tumbled down the mountainside **when the Cyclops shouted**.*

Complex Sentence Crafting

Example Recipe 10: Complex Two Dependent Clause Blocks

Crafting the Recipe

1. **Foundation Row Independent Clause**

    Odysseus fought at Troy for 10 years.

2. **Middle Row Dependent Clause**

    a. [SSV] means a clause beginning with a subordinate conjunction: <u>while</u> *Penelope suffered alone*

    b. Middle cell of middle row means [SSV] splitting between subject and verb of foundation clause. Use Punctuation Pattern 10.

    c. [RSV] means dependent clause beginning with a relative pronoun (*who, whom, whose, which, that*):

    <u>which</u> *seemed like a lifetime.*

    d. Ending cell means [RSV] at the end of the sentence. Use Punctuation Pattern 11.

Crafted Complex Sentence

*Odysseus, **while Penelope suffered alone**, fought at Troy for 10 years, **which seemed like a lifetime**.*

Sentence Craft

Example Recipe 11: Complex Three Dependent Blocks

Crafting the Recipe

1. **Foundation Row Independent Clause**

   Telemachus searched for his father.

2. **Middle Row Dependent Clause**

   a. [SSV] in beginning cell = beginning of any clause, usually the independent foundation clause.

   <u>after</u> Odysseus failed to return from the war

   b. Middle cell [RSV] means splitting position of any clause.

   <u>who</u> was born the day Odysseus left

   c. [DSVS] wild block in end cell = at end of sentence. I can choose either an [RSV] or an [SSV] series. I'll use a series of [SSV] clauses following Punctuation Pattern 2b.

   *because the kingdom was overrun by suitors,
   because he believed Odysseus still lived.*

   d. Use Punctuation Patterns 9-11 for clause boundaries.

Crafted Complex Sentence

After Odysseus failed to return from the war, Telemachus, who was born the day Odysseus left, searched for his father because the kingdom was overrun by suitors, because he believed the king still lived.

Complex Sentence Crafting

Example Recipe 12: Complex With One Master Block

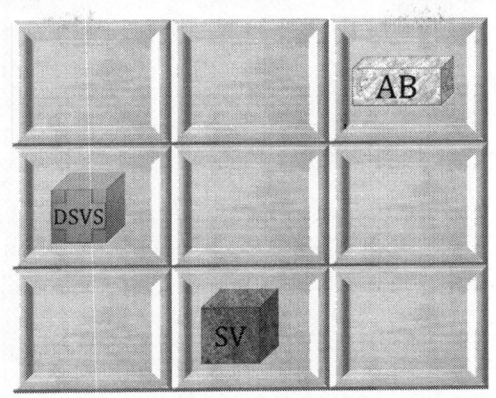

Crafting the Recipe

1. **Foundation Row Independent Clause**

    Circe changed Odysseus' men into pigs.

2. **Middle Row Dependent Clause**

    [DSVS] series wild in first cell = beginning of sentence. [RSV] blocks are not used in the beginning cell, so I will craft an [SSV] series. I will use a series of three: Pattern 2b.

    <u>after</u> they landed on her island,
    <u>when</u> they entered her palace,
    <u>as</u> they devoured her food

3. **Top Row Master Block**

    a. [AB] means absolute added to one of the clauses.
      stomachs growling
    b. End cell means [AB] placed at end of any clause. I'll place it at the end of the last clause in the [DSVS] series.
    Punctuation Pattern 5

Crafted Complex Sentence

After they landed on her island, when they entered her palace, as they devoured her food, stomachs growling, Circe changed Odysseus' men into pigs.

Sentence Craft

Example Recipe 13: Complex with Two Master Blocks

Crafting the Recipe

1. **Foundation Row Independent Clause**

    Hermes warned Odysseus of Circe's magic.

2. **Middle Row Dependent Clause**

    [SSV] in middle cell = splitting between S and V of main clause: <u>as</u> *he floated in the air*   Punctuation Pattern 10

3. **Top Row Master Block**

    a. [PAR] in middle means participle basic, phase, or series added to one of the clauses, splitting between the subject and verb. As it's best to add a phrase, that's what I'll do: <u>using</u> *his winged sandals*   Punctuation Pattern 4

    b. End cell means [APP] appositive placed at end of any clause. I'll place it at the end of the [SV]
    a <u>power</u> to transform him into an animal
    Punctuation Pattern 5

Crafted Complex Sentence

*Hermes, **as**—using his winged sandals—he floated in the air, warned Odysseus of Circe's magic, **a power to transform him into an animal**.*

Example Recipe 14: Complex Two Dependent Clauses Two Master Blocks

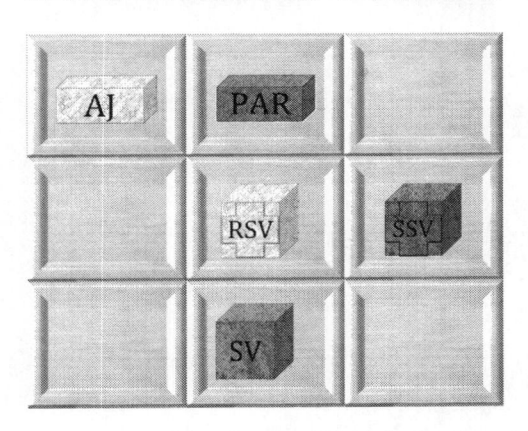

Crafting the Recipe

1. **Foundation Row Independent Clause**

    Odysseus survived the shipwreck.

2. **Middle Row Dependent Clause**

    a. [RSV] in middle cell = splitting between S and V of main clause: *who had enraged Poseidon*   Pattern 10

    b. [SSV] in end cell means at end of sentence:
       as the waves foamed around him   Pattern 11

3. **Top Row Master Block**

    a. Beginning [AJ] inserted adjective: *exhausted*   Pattern 3

    b. Middle cell [PAR] phrase splitting between subject and verb of any clause. I'll split the [SSV]:
       roaring fiercely   Punctuation Pattern 4

Crafted Complex Sentence

*Exhausted, Odysseus, **who had enraged Poseidon,** survived the shipwreck **as the waves, roaring fiercely, foamed around him.***

Sentence Craft
Complex Sentence Keystones Practice
See page 21 for instructions.

1. Topic: A ship

Practice Sentence:

Your Sentence:

Refine:
Remember: do not use a comma before an ending [SSV].

2. Topic: Santa Clause

Practice Sentence:

Your Sentence:

Refine:

3. Topic: A river

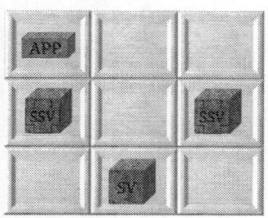

Practice Sentence:

Your Sentence:

Refine:

48 **See pg. 108 for example sentences.**

Complex Sentence Crafting

Complex Sentence Advanced Practice

4. Foundation clause: Tarzan swung through the jungle.

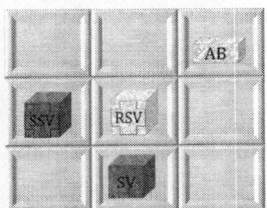

Your Sentence:

Refine: Write a series of absolute phrases.

5. Topic: Sledding

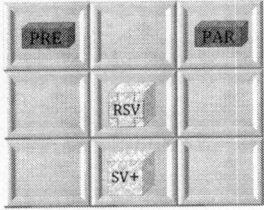

Your Sentence:

Refine: Use an essential "that" dependent clause.

6. Topic: Water skiing

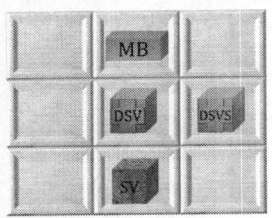

Your Sentence:

Refine:

See pg. 109 for example sentences.

Sentence Craft

Compound-Complex Sentence Crafting

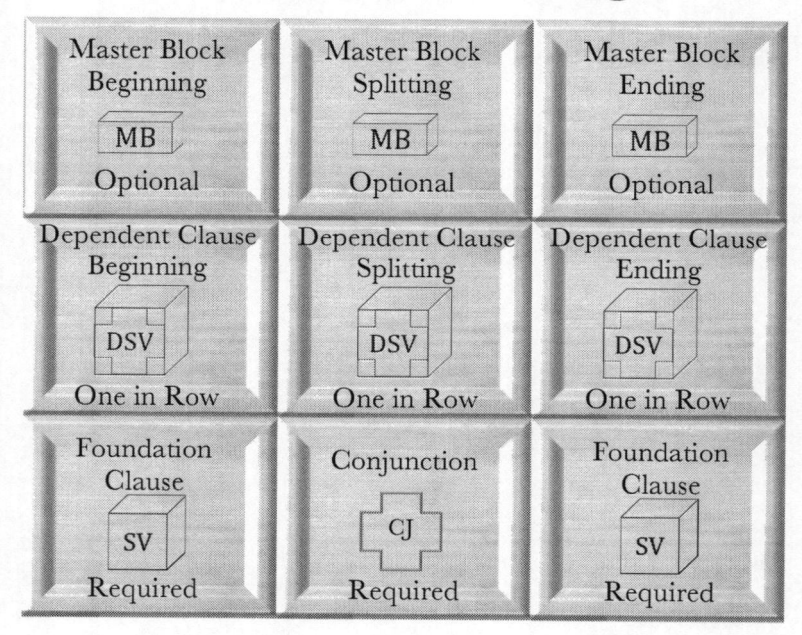

Master Block Beginning `MB` Optional	Master Block Splitting `MB` Optional	Master Block Ending `MB` Optional
Dependent Clause Beginning `DSV` One in Row	Dependent Clause Splitting `DSV` One in Row	Dependent Clause Ending `DSV` One in Row
Foundation Clause `SV` Required	Conjunction `CJ` Required	Foundation Clause `SV` Required

Compound-complex sentences encompass at least the bottom two rows of the table and often include top row master blocks as well. Due to their complexity, such sentences take a lot of time to craft. It is recommended that recipes contain no more than two dependent clauses in the middle row and no more than two master blocks in the top row. For less complex crafting, limit the middle and top rows to one block.

Compound sentences are punctuated one clause boundary at a time, following patterns 6-8 for compound boundaries and patterns 9-11 for complex boundaries. Then, if master blocks are added, they are typically surrounded by commas, following patterns 3-5.

Compound-Complex Sentence Crafting

Example Recipe 15
Compound Complex
One Dependent Clause

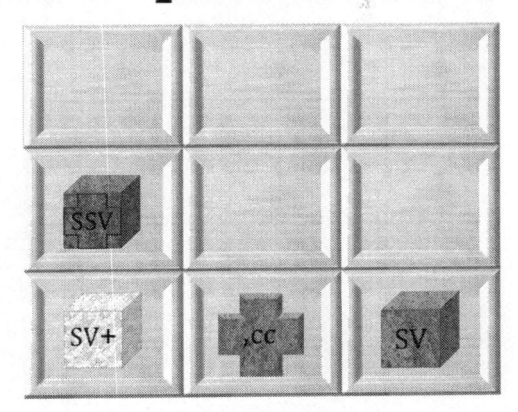

Crafting the Recipe

1. **Foundation Row: Two Independent Clauses**

    a. First clause an extended independent foundation [SV+]
    Odysseus landed, rested on Calypso's island.   Pattern 2b

    b. Second clause an [SV]
    He stayed for 10 years.

    c. Join clauses with chosen coordinating conjunction: *and* Punctuation Pattern 6.

2. **Middle Row [SSV] Dependent Clause**

    a. *After his ship sank in Poseidon's storm*

    b. [SSV] in the first cell means placing it at the beginning of a foundation clause. The crafter chooses which clause. I'll place this dependent clause before the [SV+] clause.   Pattern 9

Crafted Complex Sentence

After his ship sank in Poseidon's storm, Odysseus landed, rested on Calypso's island, and he stayed for 10 years.

Sentence Craft

Example Recipe 16
Compound Complex
Two Dependent Clauses

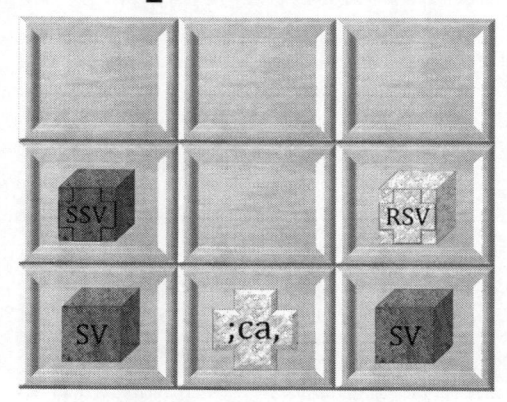

Crafting the Recipe

1. **Foundation Row: Two Independent Clauses**

    a. First clause an [SV]

    Odysseus arrived home in disguise.

    b. Second clause an [SV]

    He ambushed the suitors.

    c. Conjunction a [;ca,]: *then*   Punctuation Pattern 7

2. **Middle Row Dependent Clauses**

    a. [SSV] in beginning of a foundation clause of choice.

    <u>after</u> *20 years of war and wandering*   Pattern 9

    b. [RSV] ending a foundation clause of choice   Pattern 11

    <u>who</u> *had desecrated his home and threatened his wife*

Crafted Complex Sentence

After 20 years of war and wandering, Odysseus arrived home in disguise; then, he ambushed the suitors, **who had desecrated his home and threatened his wife.**

Compound-Complex Sentence Crafting

Example Recipe 18: Compound Complex, One Dep., One Master

Crafting the Recipe

1. **Foundation Row: Two Independent Clauses**

    a. First clause an independent foundation [SV]
    The families were feuding.

    b. Second clause an extended independent foundation [SV+]
    Romeo and Juliet fell in love.

    c. Conjunction a [;]   Punctuation Pattern 8

2. **Middle Row Dependent Clauses**

    [DSVS] splitting a foundation clause of choice. I'll use an [RSV] series this time, though I could craft an [SSV] series instead. The [RSV's] will modify Romeo and Juliet.

    who met at Capulet's party. Who chose not to hate   Pattern 10

3. **Top Row Master Block**

    [APP] splitting in clause of choice: *the Capulets and Montagues*. I'll place it in the first foundation clause, which is the [SV].   Punctuation Pattern 4

Crafted Complex Sentence
*The families, **the Capulets and Montagues**, were feuding; Romeo and Juliet, **who met at Capulet's party, who chose not to hate**, fell in love.*

Sentence Craft

Example Recipe 19: Compound Complex, Two Dep., Two Master

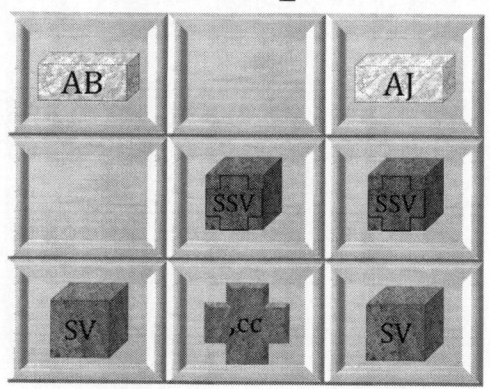

Crafting the Recipe

1. **Foundation Row: Two Independent Clauses**
    a. First [SV]: *Odysseus' journey had come to an end.*
    b. Second [SV]: *Penelope had remained faithful.*
    c. Conjunction is a [,cc]: *and*   Punctuation Pattern 6
2. **Middle Row Dependent Clauses**
    a. [SSV] splitting a foundation clause of choice
       although it had lasted decades   Punctuation Pattern 10
    b. [SSV] ending a foundation clause of choice.
       because she possessed a loyal heart   Pattern 11.
3. **Top Row Master Block**
    a. Opening [AB] with any clause: *soul weary*   Pattern 3
    b. Ending inserted [AJ] with any clause: *noble*   Pattern 5

Crafted Complex Sentence
   Although it had lasted decades, Odysseus' journey had come to an end, and, **soul weary***, Penelope had remained faithful,* **noble** *because she possessed a loyal heart.*

Compound-Complex Sentence Crafting

Compound Complex Keystones Practice

Refer to page 21 for instructions.

1. Topic: Lightening

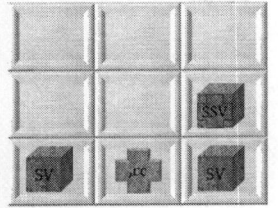

Practice Sentence:

Your Sentence:

Refine:

2. Topic: A cartoon

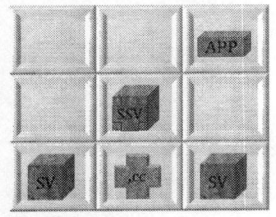

Practice Sentence:

Your Sentence:

Refine:

3. Topic: Basketball

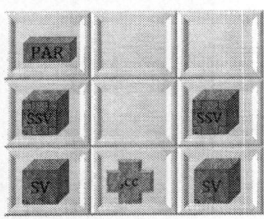

Practice Sentence:

Your Sentence:

Refine:

See pg. 108 for example sentences.

Sentence Craft
Compound Complex Advanced Practice
Refer to page 21 for instructions.

4. Topic: A dance

Your Sentence:

Refine:

5. Topic: A tsunami

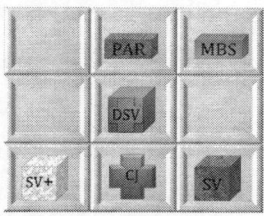

Your Sentence:

Refine: Use dashes.

6. Topic: A sea captain

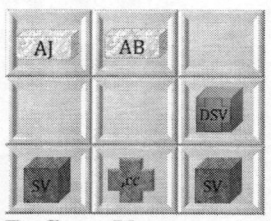

Your Sentence:

Refine: Use extended forms of master blocks.

Part II
The Ingredients

The Foundation (Bottom) Row Ingredients

Section I

Foundation / Independent Clauses

Used to Form All Sentences

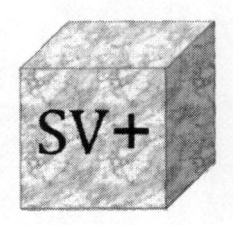

SV **SV+**

Bottom Row Ingredients

Foundation Row Terms

Clause: A group of words containing at least a subject and a verb and often a direct object or complement.

Foundation clause: A clause that can stand alone as its own sentence. Like all clauses, it has at least one subject and one verb. It is also called an **independent clause**.

Simple Sentence: A sentence containing only one foundation clause. A simple sentence is often different from a basic foundation clause because it can include multiple elements (subjects, verbs, direct objects, and complements) as well as multiple phrases but still has only one clause. Thus, all foundation clauses are simple sentences, but a simple sentence is usually a foundation clause and more.

Noun: A person, place, thing, or idea.

Pronoun: General word that substitutes for a specific noun: *I, he, she, we, us, our, they, it, who...*

Subject: The main noun or pronoun in a clause.

Verb: A word that shows the action or state of a noun.

Linking verb: A verb linking a subject to a word that renames or describes it. Linking verbs include the "to be" verbs *is, am, are, was, were, be, been, being* as well as the verbs *appears, feels, looks, seems, smells, grows.*

Complement: The word linked to the subject of a clause by a linking verb.

Direct Object: The noun receiving the action of the verb in a clause.

Phrase: A group of words that acts as a unit but does not include a subject and verb.

Preposition: A word that shows the relationship between two nouns: *at, around, across, beyond, like, of, over, to, with...*

Prepositional Phrase: Word group that starts with a preposition, ends with a noun, and usually includes one or two adjectives in-between. **Examples:** *around the world, over the barren mountains, across the sea, like me, of love.*

Sentence Craft

Foundation Clause

A foundation clause block is required for any sentence. It is the only block that can independently be its own sentence. Thus, a foundation clause is also called an **independent clause.** If used alone, it is the most basic form of **simple sentence**. The initials SV remind the crafter that every foundation clause (and thus every sentence) needs at least one subject (the main noun in a clause) and one verb and usually also includes additional words as shown in the forms below. When this block appears in a recipe, the crafter may choose one of its four basic forms.

Four basic forms

1. Subject + Verb

Steve fled.

2. Subject + Verb + Direct Object

Steve slaughtered a pig.

3. Subject + Verb + Prepositional Phrase

Steve hid in the darkness.

4. Subject + Linking Verb + Complement

Steve was lonely.

Function

The most common foundation block and the one the sentence crafter should master first. Thus, it is referred to as the **keystone** for the bottom row.

Frequency

All forms are common; however, as you strive to craft using action verbs, patterns 2 and 3, which end with a direct object or prepositional phrase, are most common.

Punctuation

Place a period at the end of an independent clause acting as its own simple sentence. See Punctuation Pattern 1.

Bottom Row Ingredients

Foundation Crafting Tips

Use Specific Nouns for Subjects/Objects

Specific nouns are best as they help paint a more descriptive picture in the reader's head. Consider the difference, for example, between *car* and *Ferrari*.

General nouns with more specific examples

Car = *Porsche, Suburban, Xterra, Volkswagen Beatle.*

Dog = *Labrador, poodle, pit bull, collie, chowchow*

Person = *convict, lawyer, doctor, nurse, administrator*

Use Specific Action Verbs

Avoid be verbs: *is, am, are, was, were, be, been, being.*

Specific action verbs paint a more descriptive movie in the reader's head. Expand your vocabulary of specific action verbs using a thesaurus.

Walked = *marched, pranced, sauntered, shuffled*

Ran = *dashed, jogged, loped, scurried, sprinted*

Pronoun Tips

Use Subject Pronouns for Subjects

I, she, he, we, they   *I* lost the battle.

Use Subject Pronouns for Complements

The winner is *he*. I am *she*! It was *I*.

Use Object Pronouns for Direct Objects

me, her, him, us, them   The argument hurt *him*.

Use Object Pronouns in Prepositional Phrases

He smiled *at her*. He wouldn't listen *to us*.

You is the Implied Subject in Commands

Forgive me. Take out the trash. Meet me in the village.

All of the above are complete foundation clauses.

Sentence Craft

Some Nouns for Subjects and Direct Objects

Climbing	mountaineer, Everest, K2, Denali, summit, face, carabineer, glacier, crevasse, moraine, crag, ice axe, avalanche, snow cave, harness, crampons
Sailing	clipper, frigate, galleon, captain, mast, sails, decks, starboard, port, bow, aft, helm, rudder, anchor, flag, skiff, dingy, lifeboat, galley, gale, crest, trough, swells, horizon, cove, port, isle, trade wind, Easterly, Westerly, doldrums.
Pirates	spy glass, plank, Jolly Roger, quarters, cannon, fort, salvo, plume, cutlass, swashbuckler, privateer, doubloon, parrot, mate, ransom, captive, hook, patch, crows nest, lookout
Island	coconut, palm tree, sand, crab, lobster, shipwreck, bottle, conch, hammock, kelp, coral, reef, shelter, hut
Weather	hurricane, surge, flood, tornado, cumulonimbus, torrent, drizzle, hail, sleet, blizzard, breeze, whiteout, frost, fog
Geology	volcano, Mount St. Helens, earthquake, Richter Scale, lava, magma, tectonic plate, ridge, Mississippi River, range, Rocky Mountains
Minecraft	Steve, villager, mob, enderman, blaze, skeleton, spider jockey, the Ender dragon, pickaxe, sword, bow, arrow, forge, ore, crafting table, mine, cave, diamond, shears, silk, wool, cliff, sugarcane, garden, cabin
Africa	savanna, lion, lioness, pride, herd, hyena, giraffe, gazelle, zebra, crocodile, waterhole, mudflat, drought
Space	meteor, comet, Mars, Pluto, Sun, Milky Way, galaxy, Hubble Telescope, satellite, International Space Station, Leo, constellation
Time	sunset, sunrise, dawn, twilight, evening, darkness, midday, noon

Bottom Row Ingredients

Some Action Verbs to Consider			
argue	discard	inhale	slip
baffle	disgruntle	liberate	slog
billow	disgust	loom	slosh
blame	dishearten	maneuver	spew
blast	dishevel	moan	spill
capture	dispute	penetrate	split
cascade	distract	plaster	spoil
chill	disturb	plummet	spring
clash	dive	pock	startle
coil	divulge	polish	stir
compel	drown	predict	stretch
conceal	efface	prevent	suggest
confound	encapsulate	pursue	supplant
contend	exhale	reveal	sweep
contort	explode	ripple	tear
correct	expound	ruin	trample
crumble	extend	save	trouble
demoralize	foil	scamper	twist
derail	frustrate	seep	unravel
detract	grant	shear	unveil
disclose	illustrate	shock	vanish
discourage	impede	shred	wear
discover	incinerate	slice	whimper

Extended Foundation Clause

SV+

Represents an independent foundation clause with a compound element: multiple subjects, verbs, direct objects, prepositional phrases, or complements. The plus sign represents the added element(s).

Function

Technically, this block is an extension of the standard foundation clause block. It simply contains more elements.

Frequency

Common

Standard Punctuation: Pattern 2

For two elements, place a conjunction without a comma between the elements.

For three or more elements, place commas between all elements, and then add a conjunction before the last element.

Creative / Informal Punctuation

Use just commas between two or more elements: Pattern 2B.
Use just conjunctions between three or more elements: 2C.

Element Series Examples

Subjects
The zombie and the mob hunted Steve in the brewing darkness.

Verbs
The creeper *hissed, screeched, trembled* as it died in the sun.

Direct objects
Steve damaged his *shoulder, knee, and ankle* in the fall.

Complements
The passage appears *dark and steep and slippery*.

Ending Prepositional Phrases
The snow avalanched *down the mountain, over the trees, and across the road*.

The Bottom Row Ingredients

Section II

Conjunctions

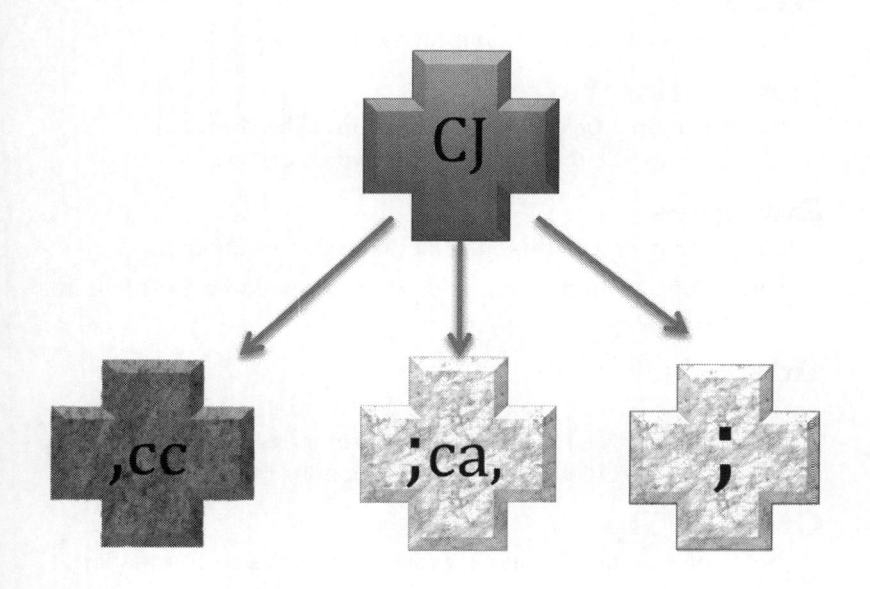

CJ

,cc   **;ca,**   **;**

Sentence Craft

Coordinating Conjunction
,cc

and, but, or, nor, for, so, yet

The most important or **keystone** compounding conjunction. The coordinating conjunction joins two foundation clauses into a compound sentence.

Function
To coordinate means to match, and to conjoin means to combine. Thus, a coordinating conjunction joins two similar elements together—in this case, independent clauses.

Frequency
The most common compounding conjunction.

Punctuation Pattern 6
Place a comma before the conjunction. The comma is unnecessary if either clause is four words or less.

Examples
The door swung softly shut, *and* I felt relieved about it.

The village lay hidden in the dale, *so* the explorers missed it in the darkness.

Other Uses
The most common coordinating conjunctions—*and, or*—are also used between elements or phrases in series. See [SV+] element series block and the series options for master blocks.

Crafting Tip
Both sides of the conjunction must be a complete foundation clause with a subject and verb or it's a simple sentence, not requiring a comma before the conjunction.

Simple: The hurricane decimated the coast and caused millions of dollars in damage. (No subject after conjunction.)

Compound: The hurricane decimated the coast, and it caused millions of dollars in damage.

Bottom Row Ingredients

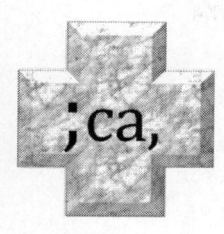

Conjunctive Adverb

;ca,

however, therefore, thus, nevertheless, then, next, consequently, furthermore, subsequently, etc.

There are many conjunctive adverbs, but the above are among the most common.

Function
Used as another way to join compound sentences.

Frequency
Medium

Punctuation Pattern 7
When joining two independent clauses, a semi-colon precedes the conjunctive adverb and a comma follows.

Examples
Steve needs a strong sword; *however,* he is out of iron.

The sun was low on the horizon; *consequently,* the enemy refused to retire.

Other Use
A conjunctive adverb can also be inserted into the middle of an independent clause as a modifier. In such a case, *however,* the adverb is surrounded by commas as in this very sentence. See top row Inserted Adverb [AV] block.

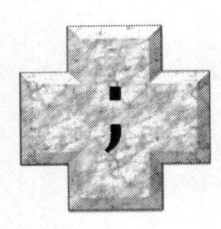

Semi-colon

A semi-colon is the only punctuation mark with the power to join two foundation clauses all on its own.

Function
The semi-colon is interchangeable with the period, but a period divides two clauses while a semi-colon joins them with only a short pause.

Frequency
Compared to other compounding conjunctions, semi-colons are relatively rare.

Punctuation Pattern 8
Place between two independent clauses.
Example
The end has come; my game has crashed.

Other Uses:

Clause Element Series: A semi-colon can also be used to separate categories in a multi-category series as in the following example:

Steve carried *water, ale, and jerky; an axe, a sword and a bow; and a crafting table of fine workmanship.*

Bottom Row Ingredients

Conjunction Wild

When the conjunction wild appears in a recipe, the sentence crafter may choose any of the three compounding conjunctions with the appropriate punctuation:

coordinating conjunction
and, but, or, nor, for, so, yet

conjunctive adverb with semi-colon and comma
however, therefore, thus, nevertheless, then, next, consequently, furthermore, subsequently, etc.

semi-colon ;

Function

Compounding conjunctions join two foundation clauses together to form a compound sentence. Iron wild blocks like this one allow more flexibility for the sentence crafter when desired.

Frequency

Coordinating conjunctions are the most common.

Conjunctive adverbs are fairly common.

Semi-colons are rare compared to other conjunctions.

Punctuation Patterns 6-8

Punctuate according to chosen conjunction.

Examples

Coordinating Conjunction

Captain Blakely hoisted the white flag, *and* the shore cannons stopped firing.

Conjunctive adverb

Captain Blakely hoisted the white flag; *consequently*, the shore cannons stopped firing.

Semi-colon

Captain Blakely hoisted the white flag; the shore cannons stopped firing.

Sentence Craft

The Middle Row Ingredients

Dependent Clauses

Used to Form Complex Sentences

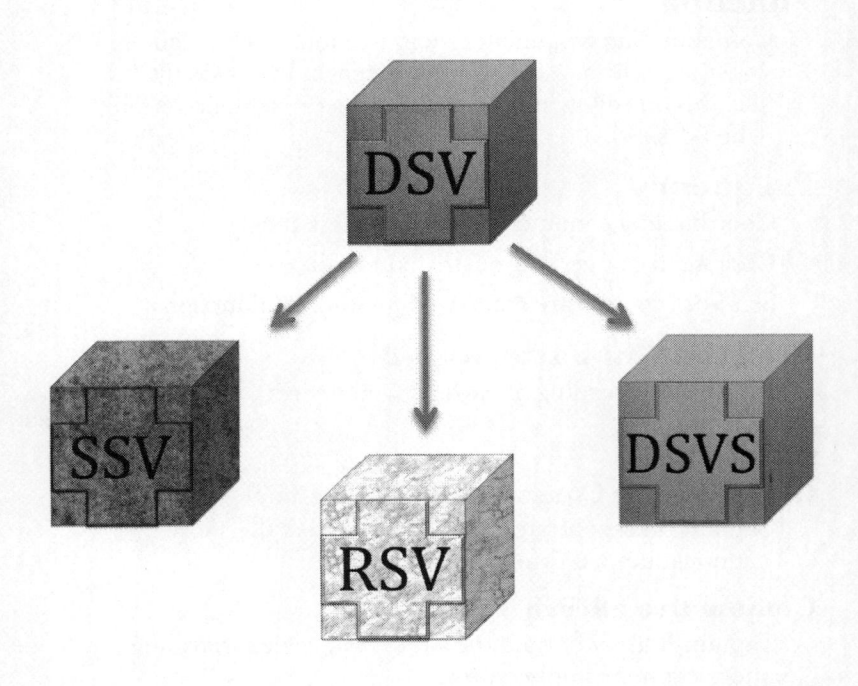

Middle Row Ingredients: Dependent Clauses

Middle Row Terminology

Complex sentence: A sentence formed when one or more dependent clauses are connected to an independent foundation clause.

Dependent clause: Like all clauses, a dependent clause has at least a subject and a verb, but it cannot stand as an independent sentence. It must be connected to an independent clause to form a sentence. It always begins with a subordinating conjunction or relative pronoun.

Subordinate dependent clause: A clause that starts with a subordinating conjunction. The word subordinate means secondary or less important. A subordinate clause is considered secondary to the independent clause it is connected to. **Example:** *If you practice hard*, you can master these terms.

Subordinating conjunction: *after, although, as, because, before, even though, if, since, though, unless, until, when, whenever, where, wherever, whereas, while.* **Subordinating** because it makes a clause less important or secondary, and **conjunction** because it joins a dependent clause to an independent one.

Relative dependent clause: A clause with a relative pronoun as its subject. Like all dependent clauses, it cannot stand alone but must be connected to an independent foundation clause to make sense. **Example:** Brutus, *who was a traitor*, abandoned Cesar in his time of need.

Relative pronoun: Act as the subject of a relative dependent clause: *who, whom, whose, which, that*

Sentence Craft

Subordinate Clause

Place a subordinating conjunction at the beginning of an independent foundation clause to form a subordinate clause.

Important: Unlike foundation clauses, dependent clauses like the subordinate clause cannot form a sentence alone. Instead, a dependent clause must be joined to an independent foundation clause to form a **complex sentence**.

Subordinating Conjunctions

after, although, as, because, before, even though, if, since, though, unless, until, when, whenever, where, wherever, whereas, while.

Function

Row 2 Keystone: The [SSV] is the most important dependent clause block.

Frequency

The most common dependent clause.

Punctuation Patterns 9-11

Place a comma immediately after a subordinate clause that begins a sentence.

Place commas before and after a subordinate clause in the splitting position of a sentence.

Usually no comma is used before a subordinate clause that ends a sentence.

Examples

Beginning: *Unless Thorin makes peace with the elves*, the dwarves will never see daylight again.

Splitting: Bilbo, *when the battle heated up*, turned invisible.

Ending: The eagles appeared *when the battle seemed lost*.

Middle Row Ingredients: Dependent Clauses

Subordinate Clause Crafting Tips

One way to craft a subordinate clause is to start with a foundation clause in any of its four forms and then add a subordinating conjunction. Then, craft a new foundation clause and connect it to your subordinating clause to form a complex sentence.

Pattern	Independent Foundation Clause	Subordinate Dependent Clause
S+V	Taran hid.	*Because* Taran hid
S+V+DO	Gurgi stole food.	*While* Gurgi stole food
S+V+PRE	Doli disappeared into the forest.	*After* Doli disappeared in the forest
S+LV+C	Henwen is a pig.	*Although* Henwen is a pig

Complex Sentence Examples

Beginning Crafting Example

    S   V   S   V

Because Taran hid, the Horned King rode past.

Splitting Crafting Examples

S   S   V DO   V

Taran—*while Gurgi stole food*—slept.

S   S   LV C   V   V   PRE

Taran, *although Henwen was a pig*, would die for her.

Ending Crafting Example

   S   V   S   V   V   PRE

The battle raged *after Doli had disappeared into the forest*.

Sentence Craft

Relative Pronoun Dependent Clause

A relative pronoun dependent clause has a subject and verb but must be connected to a foundation clause to form a sentence. It begins with a **relative pronoun,** which usually acts as the subject of the clause. An [RSV] is also referred to as an **adjective clause** because it always modifies an adjacent noun.

Relative pronouns
who, whom, whose, which, that

Function
Form complex sentences and add information to nouns.

Frequency
Less common than subordinating dependent clauses.

Important Terminology and Punctuation
Essential: A clause that helps to further specify exactly which noun is being discussed.

Non-essential: A clause that simply adds additional information.

Punctuation Patterns 9-11
Do not use commas with essential clauses.

Use commas with non-essential clauses.

If in doubt, place commas only if a pause seems necessary.

Middle Row Ingredients: Dependent Clauses

Relative Dependent Clause Crafting Tips

Do not use commas with *that* relative clauses
That clauses are usually essential (necessary).

Use commas with *which* relative clauses
Which clauses are usually non-essential (unnecessary).

Use *who* to begin clauses modifying people
Eric, *who left yesterday*, is my brother.

Use *which* or *that* to begin clauses modifying things
The computer, *which came in the mail yesterday*, broke.

Complex Sentence Examples

Note: Beginning relative clauses are awkward and not implemented in Sentence Craft, although it is possible to write a rare type of inverted sentence using the relative pronoun *that*, such as in this example: *That the storm has ended*, it is true. Nevertheless, such sentences become overly awkward when combined with other blocks.

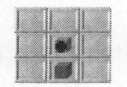

Splitting Crafting Examples

                 S   V   DO
Essential: The man *who stole my food* is a convict.
                          S V   PRE
Non-essential: My only sister, *who died in January*, hated commas.

Ending Crafting Examples

                                   S   V   DO
Essential: Look out for the Camaro *that squealed its tires*.
                     S   V
Phillip knew *that victory went to the strong*.
                                 S   LV   DO
Non-essential: Garth lost his hat, *which was a tragedy*.

Sentence Craft

Dependent Clause Wild

DSV

When the dependent wild appears in a recipe, the sentence crafter may choose either a subordinate dependent clause [SSV] or a relative pronoun clause [RSV].

Function

Forms a complex sentence when connected to an independent clause. Iron wild blocks like this one allow more flexibility for the sentence crafter when desired.

Punctuation Patterns 9-11

Depends upon chosen dependent clause and context. See subordinate dependent clauses and relative dependent clauses for examples.

Typical Punctuation

Beginning

Place a comma immediately after the dependent clause.

Splitting

Place commas before and after a dependent clause that splits between the subject and the verb in the main clause or is otherwise placed in the middle of a sentence.

Ending

Typically, you should not use a comma before an ending dependent clause; however, sometimes this rule is violated if a writer desires a pause before the clause.

Middle Row Ingredients: Dependent Clauses

Dependent Clause Wild Series

DSVS

When the dependent wild series appears in a recipe, the sentence crafter may choose either a subordinate dependent clause or a relative one to write in series.

Function
Forms a complex sentence with multiple dependent clauses in series connected to an independent clause. Iron wild blocks like this one allow more flexibility for the sentence crafter when desired.

Punctuation
Punctuate the boundaries between the dependent clause(s) and the independent clause the same way you would with dependent clauses used singly. Then, place commas or conjunctions between the series dependent clauses depending on desired affect.

Crafting Tips
To write a dependent clause wild series, simply place two or three dependent clauses side by side. You may repeat the same subordinating conjunction / relative pronoun or use different ones.

Same Subordinating Conjunction or Relative Pronoun
When the stallion galloped away, *when* the mare pursued with a neigh, I knew I had to have a horse.
WWII had ended, *which* meant Grandpa could come home, *which* meant he would soon meet Grandma.

Different Sub. Conjunction or Relative Pronoun
Mr. Holmes stepped into the street *as* the trolley careened down 5th Avenue *because* its breaks had failed.

Sentence Craft

Dependent Clause Series Examples

Beginning Crafting Example

Although the father had read regularly, because the son did not read, the books sat abandoned on the shelf.

While General Grant sent wave after wave of troops at the Confederate lines and while hundreds of cannon roared, Jeb Stuart's cavalry slipped away.

Splitting Crafting Examples

Boo Radley, *who wanted to prove his worth, who legitimately cared for his neighbors*, saved Jem's life.

The lion *that had watched from its cage, that had eyed Yolanda hungrily*, escaped yesterday.

Ending Crafting Example

The battle raged *after Smaug had disappeared into the sky because the sun had not yet set*.

Bilbo also disappeared *as the elves attacked the dwarves, as the orcs and wargs appeared on the horizon*.

Top Row Ingredients: Master Blocks

The Top Row Ingredients

Master Blocks

Used to Polish and Refine All Sentences

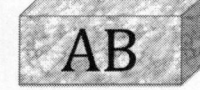

- MB
- PRE
- PAR
- APP
- AB
- AJ
- AV
- MBS

Sentence Craft

Master Block Wild

A **master block** is a word or phrase added to or extending a sentence. Master blocks are the tools of the master craftsman, the techniques used by professional writers to separate their sentences from those of amateurs. When this wild block appears in a recipe, the sentence crafter may choose which block from the options below. Each block is explained in more detail in the pages that follow. The first three blocks below are the keystone master blocks. Once you master these, you can add the three marble blocks to your crafting repertoire.

Prepositional Phrase
  Basic, Extended, or Series

Participle
  Basic, Extended, or Series

Appositive
  Basic, Extended, or Series

Absolute
  Basic, Extended, or Series

Inserted Adjective
  Basic, Extended, or Series

Inserted Adverb
  Basic, Extended, or Series

Top Row Ingredients: Master Blocks

Master Block Crafting Tips
Crafting Options

Every master block has three options that the sentence crafter may use when a block is included in a recipe: **basic, extended, and series**. If desired, a recipe writer can provide instructions requesting a particular option in the refine field at the bottom of the crafting table. The recipe writer might, for example, request that any master block take the extended form. Otherwise, the sentence crafter is free to choose which form to use.

Basic: The basic option is a master block's most simple form. In most cases, the basic form is a single word, though with prepositional phrases, it is the most simple form of phrase.

Extended: Master blocks can be extended by adding additional modifying words. Prepositional phrases, for example, can be extended by adding additional adjectives; thus, the basic prepositional phrase *on the sea* could be extended to *on the deep blue sea*. A basic participle (e.g. *blazing*) can be extended by adding a prepositional phrase: *blazing <u>through the forest</u>*.

Series: A series is a list. Crafters can make lists of either basic or extended master block forms. Master block series forms are typically two or three elements long. Crafting in series adds rhythm to sentences and can be done in all forms of writing.

Punctuation Patterns 3-5

Although there are exceptions, typically commas should be placed on the boundaries of master blocks. The sentence crafter can think of these commas as acting like parenthesis that indicate to the reader that the word, phrase, or series has been inserted into the beginning, middle, or end of a clause.

Dashes—singly or in pairs—can also be used to set off master blocks from the rest of the sentence—making the pause more pronounced.

Parenthesis can be used also (creating a softer affect).

Sentence Craft

Prepositional Phrase
Preposition+ Adjective(s) + Noun

Preposition: A word that shows the relationship between two nouns. A preposition is placed **pre**vious to a noun. The preposition and its noun plus any adjectives in between forms the phrase. **Example phrases:**
across the river, over the hill, to Athens, beyond the plain

Extended Prepositional Phrase Options
A. Add adjective(s): *by the hill* ➔ *by the barren, rocky hill*

B. Chain together multiple phrases:
Behind the ghost ➔ *behind the ghost in the land of Nod.*

Common Prepositions

aboard	behind	**in**	past
about	below	inside	**to**
above	beneath	instead of	through
across	beside	into	throughout
after	besides	**like**	toward
against	between	near	under
alongside	beyond	**of**	until
amid	**by**	off	unto
among	despite	**on**	up
apart from	down	onto	upon
around	during	opposite	**with**
at	except	out	within
because of	**for**	outside	without
before	from	**over**	

Function and Frequency
Commonly used to end an S + V + PRE foundation clause.
Commonly used to extend other master blocks.
A "like" prepositional phrase often forms a simile.

Punctuation Patterns 3-5
Beginning: Follow with a comma in most cases.
Splitting: Surround by commas, parenthesis, or dashes if inserted/non-essential, making a pause appropriate.
Ending: Usually essential so no punctuation is used.

Top Row Ingredients: Master Blocks

Prepositional Phrase Crafting Tips

Essential prep. phrases do not need commas
The skeleton *with the eye patch* shot Steve.

Use object pronouns (me, us, them)
No: Give it to *I*. **Yes:** Give it to *me*.

How to Remember Most Prepositions
Start with two nouns such as a *squirrel* and a *bridge*. Any word that shows their relationship is a preposition. A rat can run *over*, *across*, or *beneath* and sit *beside* a bridge.

Memorize these common prepositions
At, by, in, like, to, of, with

Beginning Crafting Examples

Basic: *Into the darkness*, Odysseus descended.

Extended: *Into the darkness of the Underworld*, he went.

Series: *Beyond the known world*, *across the troubled sea*, *among the forbidden isles*, the King of Achaea wandered.

Splitting Crafting Examples

Basic: Prometheus, *like an angel*, gave fire to men.

Extended: Prometheus, *like a saving angel*, gave men fire.

Series: Zeus, *in shock*, *with rage*, punished Prometheus.

Ending Crafting Examples

Phrase: Zeus chained Prometheus *to a cliff*.

Extended: Zeus chained Prometheus *to a cliff on a barren mountain by a ravenous eagle*.

Series: Hercules freed Prometheus *from the eagle*, *from the chains*, *and from Zeus' vengeful grip*. (Sometimes the same preposition is repeated, sometimes not.)

Sentence Craft

PAR
Ing Participle or Participial Phrase

Participle = verb + ing
A participle is a type of adjective (meaning it describes a noun) formed by adding a suffix to the end of a verb. The "ing" ending present participle is the relevant one here.

Participial Phrase = Participle + Modifiers

Variations

Participle + Adverb
Flying swiftly, the bird vanished.

Participle + Adjective
The soldier, *looking dazed*, collapsed.

Participle + Noun
The volcano erupted, *spewing lava*.

Participle + Prepositional phrase
The dragon appeared, *grinning at the dwarves*.

Function: Part adjective and part verb, participles and participial phrases add both description and action to the subjects and direct objects they modify.

Frequency
Single participles are rare, especially in formal writing, but participial phrases are common. Like all adjectives, participles and their phrases should be used sparingly.

Punctuation Patterns 3-5
Beginning: Follow with a comma or dash.

Splitting: Usually surround by commas or dashes except for an "essential" phrase that further clarifies which noun is being discussed: The girl *carrying the purse* is his girlfriend.

Ending: Use a comma or dash except with an essential phrase that modifies the direct object instead of the subject of the foundation clause as in this example:

The lion left the carcass *rotting on the savannah*.

Top Row Ingredients: Master Blocks
Participle and Phrase Crafting Tips
1. **"Ing" words by "to be" verbs are not participles**
   "Participles" or phrases directly before or after "to be" verbs (*is, am, are, was, be, been, being*) function as nouns and verbs, not inserted participles, **unless in the splitting position**.
   Noun (no): *Swimming in mud* is my pig's favorite activity.
   Verb (no): Locusts were *invading* the farm.
   Participle (yes): Erik, *dodging darts*, was frightened.
2. **Avoid awkward or misplaced phrases**
   Unclear: Elves ambushed the trolls *wielding swords*.
   Better: Elves ambushed the trolls, *wielding swords*.
   The comma indicates the phrase modifies elves not trolls.
   Or: Elves, *wielding swords*, ambushed the trolls.

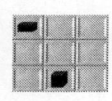

Beginning Crafting Examples

Single: *Dodging*, Aragorn leapt up the ramparts.
Phrase: *Paddling solemnly*, the travelers reached shore.
Series: *Groping for a hold, reaching vainly*, Gandalf fell.

Splitting Crafting Examples

Single: Bilbo, *reminiscing*, remembered the journey.
Phrase: Smaug, *roaring with rage*, attacked the village.
Series: Fili, *ducking* and *dodging*, avoided the blows.

Ending Crafting Examples

Single: The eagles appeared in the sky, *screeching*.
Phrase: The eagles saved the day, *swooping upon the orcs*.
Series: Bilbo showed gratitude, *embracing the eagles, praising their bravery, celebrating the victory*.

Sentence Craft

APP Appositive

A basic appositive is a noun that further identifies an adjacent noun. Typically a basic appositive will be preceded by an article adjective: *a*, *the*, or *a*.

Examples: The boat, *a cutter*, slipped into port.
The pheasant, *a rooster*, disappeared into the brush.

Extended Variation: Appositive Phrase

An appositive phrase is an appositive + modifying words and/or prepositional phrases.

Examples with appositive noun underlined:

The boat, *a <u>cutter</u> with billowed sails*, slipped into port.

The pheasant, *a plump <u>rooster</u> with blazing plumage*, disappeared into the brush.

Function and Frequency

Appositives further identify a noun in a sentence. Both basic and extended versions are common in all types of writing.

Punctuation Patterns 3-5

Beginning appositives are followed by a comma or dash.

Splitting appositives are surrounded by commas or dashes.

Ending appositives are preceded by a comma or dash.

Top Row Ingredients: Master Blocks

Appositive and Phrase Crafting Tips

1. Use this formula to find an appositive.
The/a __(noun)__ is a ____x____.

Begin with any noun in the foundation sentence.
Foundation: Willy sailed to the island.

Willy is a _x_ = boy, rascal, rebel, patriot, adventurer
The island is a _x_ = land, place, realm, kingdom, country

> **Sentence with appositives:** Willy, *an adventurer*, sailed to the island, *a forbidden realm*.

2. Craft a splitting before a beginning appositive.
If having trouble crafting an opening appositive, craft a splitting one first and then rearrange the sentence.

Beginning Crafting Examples

Basic: *Nomads*, the Arabians wandered through the Sahara.

Phrase: *A mysterious creature*, the Enderman can disappear.

Series: *A deadly enemy, an explosive foe*, creepers should be avoided in Minecraft.

Splitting Crafting Examples

Basic: TNT, *an explosive*, is dangerous.

Phrase: Steve, *the hero of Minecraft*, broke the door easily.

Series: Sheep, *vulnerable animals, tasty beasts*, live here.

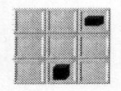

Ending Crafting Examples

Basic: Lava flowed into my hideout, *a cave*.

Phrase: The mine cart crashed on the track, *a steep course*.

Series: The volcano erupted, *a shock, a tragedy*.

Sentence Craft

Absolute

A **basic absolute** is a pair of words formed by placing a participle or other adjective after a noun. **Examples:** *hands worn, toes frozen, heart aching*

Extended Absolutes

Extended absolutes are actually more common than the basic noun + participle or adjective combination.

Extended Variations

1. **Add adjectives to beginning and/or end**
   hands worn *raw*
   wrinkled toes frozen *solid*

2. **Start with a possessive pronoun (his, her, my, its, our, their)**
   his hands worn
   their toes frozen solid

3. **Add a prepositional phrase to the end:**
   hands worn *from labor*
   toes frozen *by frost*

4. **A combination of all of the above:**
   his hands worn raw *from labor*
   their wrinkled toes frozen *solid by frost.*

Function and Frequency

Absolutes add additional description to a sentence and are common, especially in informal writing, and especially in the extended form.

Punctuation Patterns 3-5

Beginning absolutes are followed by commas or dashes.
Splitting absolutes are surrounded by commas or dashes.
Ending absolutes are preceded by a comma or dash.

Top Row Ingredients: Master Blocks

Absolute Crafting Tips

1. Start with a noun. Example: *stallion*
2. Identify a specific noun that is part of the prior noun.
3. Add a participle or other adjective describing the second noun. Example: *flashing*
4. Combine the second noun and the adjective/participle into an absolute: *hooves flashing*
5. Extend by adding adjectives, personal pronouns, and/or prepositional phrases: *his hooves flashing in the distance*.
5. Craft a sentence using the first noun as the subject.
6. **Sentence:** The stallion, *his hooves flashing in the distance*, raced to the finish.

Absolute Test

If you add a "be verb" like *is*, *was*, or *were* to an absolute, a complete sentence (S + LV + C) is formed.
Example: *lights blinking*   **Test:** Lights were blinking.

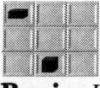

Beginning Crafting Examples

Basic: *Heart beating*, Ray scaled the fence.
Extended: *His heart beating*, **Ray scaled the fence.**
Series: *Tires spinning*, exhaust smoking, the 4 x 4 skidded.

Splitting Crafting Examples

Basic: Amy, *arms flailing*, fell into the sea.
Extended: Amy, *her arms flailing wildly*, fell into the sea.
Series: Officer Robins—*siren blaring, engine revving, pedal floored*—pursued the Mustang.

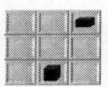

Ending Crafting Examples

Basic: Bonnie and Clyde fled, *guns blazing*.
Extended: The convicts fled, *their guns blazing in the dark*.
Series: He finished the book, *cover worn, pages torn*.

Sentence Craft

Inserted Adjective

Adjectives modify nouns. In English, adjectives are typically placed before nouns in a sentence. However, an inserted adjective is placed in an unusual spot (such as after the noun), creating a pause.

Example Adjectives
small, silent, sacred, yellow, ancient, pleasant, idealistic

Inserted Example
The weather, *pleasant*, reminded me of home.

Non-*ing* participle Adjectives (Verb + suffix)
tired, rested, agitated, excited, shaken, spent, etc.

Inserted "Non-ing" Past Participle Example
Gandalf, *flustered*, argued with Thorin.

Extended Option
Inserted adjectives can be extended by adding modifying adverbs or prepositional phrases.

Example
Gandalf, <u>*flustered* by the dwarf's greed</u>, argued with Thorin.

Function and Frequency
Insertion creatively forms a unique sentence most appropriate for informal, creative, and narrative writing—contexts where the technique is common.

Punctuation Patterns 3-5
Beginning: Follow with a comma or dash.
Splitting: Surround with commas or dashes.
Ending: Precede with a comma or dash.

Top Row Ingredients: Master Blocks

Inserted Adjective Crafting Tips

Adjective Test Tip: Place it before a noun first
The/a ___x___ noun. x=adjective. The <u>silent</u> villager.

Inserted: The villager, *silent*, wandered home.

Stuck? Try a non-ing Participle
"Non-ing" past participles, such as those ending in *ed*, are often easier to insert than standard adjectives.

Don't Confuse Inserted ed Participles with Verbs
If the sentence does not make sense with the "ed" word removed, most likely the word is a necessary verb.

Verb: He was *tired* of the war. He of the war? (Makes no sense.)

Participle: He, *tired*, left the war. He left the war. (It's ok.)

Beginning Crafting Examples

Basic: *Shaken*, Captain Dixon wept.

Extended: *Shaken by the losses*, Captain Dixon wept.

Series: *Shaken, shocked, dismayed*, Captain Dixon wept.

Splitting Crafting Examples

Basic: Caleb, *lost*, consulted his map.

Extended: Caleb, *lost in the wilderness*, consulted his map.

Series: Caleb, *lost, afraid*, consulted his map.

Ending Crafting Examples

Phrase: Chief Joseph surrendered, *heartbroken*.

Extended: Chief Joseph surrendered—*heartbroken by the sufferings of his people*.

Series: Chief Joseph surrendered, *heartbroken and weary*.

Sentence Craft

Inserted Adverb

Adverbs modify verbs, adjectives, and other adverbs. They answer the questions why, when, how, and to what extent.

Adverbs that explain **how** something happened end in "ly": *slowly, swiftly, softly, quickly, carefully, rarely, unfortunately...*

Other adverbs say **when** something happened or will happen: *yesterday, tomorrow, soon, later, afterward*

Conjunctive Adverbs can also be inserted in a clause: *however, therefore, thus, consequently, nevertheless, then...*

Extended Option

Although extending is uncommon, an inserted adverb can be extended by adding a prepositional phrase, adjective, participle, or phrase.

Brightly through the darkness, secretly hiding, suddenly changed

Conjunctive adverbs cannot be extended.

Function

Inserted adverbs are used for creative purposes such as emphasizing the adverb used or creating sentence variety. Conjunctive adverbs act as transitions.

Frequency

Inserted adverbs are most common in the single or series form. They are rarely extended.

Adverbs are common in all writing; however, they should be used sparingly. Inserted adverbs are more common in informal writing than formal writing.

Conjunctive adverbs are the most common form for inserting in the splitting position between the subject and verb of a clause.

Punctuation Patterns 3-5

Use standard insertion patterns with commas or dashes to set the adverbs off from clause in which they are inserted.

Top Row Ingredients: Master Blocks

Inserted Adverb Crafting Tips

Single adverbs are not technically *inserted* when placed immediately before or after the verb unless they are conjunctive. A series of adverbs, however, can be placed immediately before or after the verb.

Not inserted (too close to verb)
The arrow flew *swiftly*. The arrow *swiftly* flew.

To Make Inserted
Move before subject: *Swiftly*, the arrow flew.

Use conjunctive adverb: The arrow, *however*, flew swiftly.

Add a prepositional phrase between the verb and the adverb:
The arrow flew <u>into the dark</u>, *swiftly*.

Beginning Crafting Examples

Basic: *Quietly*, the thief slipped inside.

Extended: *Quietly through the dark*, the thief sneaked inside.

Series: *Wildly, angrily*, the prisoner raved like a lunatic.

Splitting Crafting Examples

Basic: The Joker, *however*, failed.

Extended: The Joker, *fortunately for Batman*, failed.

Series: The deer, *slowly and cautiously*, crossed the gorge.

Ending Crafting Examples

Phrase: Zeus overthrew the Titans, *slyly*.

Extended: Zeus overthrew the Titans, *slyly scheming*. (Extending with a participle is appropriate.)

Series: The bell tolled, *loudly, resolutely, endlessly*.

Sentence Craft

MBS — Master Block Series Wild

All master blocks can be crafted in series. When this block appears, choose any master block [PRE], [PAR], [APP], [AB], [AJ], or [AV] and write a series of two or three in a row. See each master block page for series examples.

Function

Using a word or phrase in series adds rhythm, description, and action at the same time.

Frequency

Series options are common in all forms of writing.

Standard Punctuation and Conjunctions
Series Boundaries

Place a comma or a dash after a series beginning a sentence. Surround a non-essential spitting series with commas or dashes.
Place a comma or dash before a non-essential ending series.
Note: Dashes are rare.

Standard Interior Punctuation

For a two-part series, use a conjunction without a comma between the elements.
For three or more elements place commas between all elements, but add a conjunction and a comma before the last element.

Standard Punctuation/Conjunction Examples: Pattern 2 Combined with 3-5

Two Elements: The light, *like a fleeting phantom, like a waning moon*, disappeared in the foggy darkness. [PRE]

Three Elements: The chipmunk, *nose twitching, teeth gnawing, claws scratching*, raided the tent. [AB]

Dashes on Boundaries

The man—*a mysterious spy, a strange European, and a deadly enemy*—disappeared into the crowd. [APP]

Top Row Ingredients: Master Blocks

Master Block Series Crafting Tips: Creative (Non-Standard) Punctuation

Use Only Commas Between Elements

Series of Two
Beginning: *Hoping, praying*, the climber fell. [PAR]

Splitting: The steamboat, *dark, abandoned*, drifted down the Mississippi. [AJ]

End: The volcano erupted—*spewing lava, belching fire*. [AB]

Series of Three
Beginning: *Galloping across the countryside, stirring up clouds of dust, searching through forest and glen*—the riders pursued the elusive spies. [PAR]

Splitting: Cody's yacht, *sails furled, masts straining, bow slicing through the swells*, melted into the buttery horizon. [AB].

End: Antony sneaked into the compound, *slipping through the shadows, avoiding the guards, searching for Bathsheba*. [PAR]

Use Only Conjunctions Between Elements

Series of Two
Beginning: *Eyes peeled and heart troubled*, the security guard approached the door. [AB]

Splitting: The mist, *sinking and drifting*, blanketed the valley. [PAR]

End: The diver waited, *confident and poised and still*. [AJ]

Series of Three
Beginning: *Slowly and deliberately and skillfully*, Hillary ascended toward the summit. [AV]

Splitting: The bat—*dodging quickly and screeching loudly and eating heartily*—hunted through the darkness. [PAR]

End: I ate the chicken, *slurping and gurgling and gagging*. [PAR]

Tips for Teaching
Sentence Craft

Teaching Tips
Sample Unit

One way to begin teaching Sentence Craft is with a 12-15 day immersive unit to introduce the keystones and four sentence types. Plan for about 20-30 minutes per day in the beginning, less time as students improve. You may choose to introduce marble and iron blocks as you go along, or save these until after you have covered keystones. If time is limited, you may choose to skip marble and iron blocks altogether.

I. Practice Simple Sentence Recipe Keystones

[SV] +CC [SSV]   PRE PAR APP

Day 1
Introduce students to the handbook, including the objectives on page 10, the quick reference ingredients list on pages 11-13, and the sentence crafting instructions on page 22. Also show how it is divided into two parts: Part I for sentence crafting and Part II for details about the ingredient blocks, including crafting tips.

Day 2
-Go over pages 23-24 to introduce students to simple sentences, the [SV] block, and the simple sentence table.

-Together as a class craft the recipe on page 25. Also, show students the information on pages 60-63.

-Time permitting, you may wish to have each student write four sentences of their own, each following one of the four possible [SV] patterns.

Days 3-5
-Refer to page 99 for specific tips on the daily crafting process.
-If desired, you may wish to introduce the [SV+] marble block at this time and substitute it for the [SV] block in one of the recipes on page 31.
-Introduce the [PRE], [PAR], and [APP] top row keystones one day at a time, crafting page 31 recipes 1, 2, and 3, respectively. Students should refer to the ingredients section of the handbook for specific information and crafting examples for each block.
-Students should refer to punctuation patterns 3-5 on page 16. Save the advanced recipes on page 32 for later.

Sentence Craft

II. Practice Compound Sentence Keystone
Days 6-9

-Introduce the compound crafting table on page 33, emphasizing how the bottom row differs from the simple sentence table.

-Introduce the [,cc] keystone conjunction block.

-You may want to also introduce the [;ca,] and [;] marble blocks as they all can be used interchangeably as compounding conjunctions [CJ].

-Have students complete the recipes on page 39, substituting other conjunction blocks for the [,cc] if desired. Save page 40 for advanced crafting later.

-Students should refer to page 21 for crafting instructions. Note, students do not have to follow the *exact* order of the instructions, for there are different ways to reach a similar final product.

III. Practice Complex Sentences
Days 10-12

-Introduce students to the complex crafting table on page 41.

-Introduce students to the [SSV] block. Have them read pages 72-73 in the ingredients section.

-Have students craft the first recipes on page 48, one per day. They should refer to page 21 for instructions and to punctuation patterns 9-11 on page 17.

-You may also choose to introduce the [RSV] block at this time. If so, replace an [SSV] in Recipe 3 with an [RSV].

IV. Compound-Complex Sentences

-Introduce students to the compound-complex crafting table on page 50. As with all sentence types, top row master blocks are optional.

-Have students craft the keystone recipes on page 55. They should refer to page 21 for instructions.

V. Incorporate Marble and Wild Blocks

Introduce marble and wild blocks with various sentence types using the second page of each activity sheet.

Teaching Tips

Daily Sentence Craft Process

Outlined below is the typical daily process to follow. Each day have the entire class craft a sentence based on a recipe from the handbook, the optional Power Point available online, or the online random generator. Find links to the latter two at sentencecraft.blogspot.com. Begin with simple sentences and keystones before moving to compound and complex sentences as well as marble and iron blocks. See the example unit on the previous two pages for scope and sequence tips.

Teacher Models

As the teacher, model how to craft a recipe of that type of sentence. As you model, teach students to refer to the quick reference guide at the beginning of the handbook or the ingredients section for more specific details about the blocks. Also teach them to refer to page 21 for crafting instructions and to the example crafted recipes in each section. Students should write the class sentence in the "Practice Sentence" space next to the recipe on their activity sheets.

You may wish to work to the point where a capable student or assigned groups of students will model the full-class daily practice recipe instead of you.

Students Craft Their Own Sentences

Next, each student should craft his or her own sentence, either independently or in small groups, based on the same recipe the class just practiced. They should write the new sentence in the adjacent "Own Sentence" space. You may have students do this as homework if time is limited.

Students Peer Review With Partners

Next, students should peer review and sign each other's sentences, providing constructive criticism as necessary. They should check for specific nouns and action verbs, correct use of master blocks, and punctuation.

Students Share With Class

Time permitting, have students help you identify some of the best sentences and have the writers share them with the class.

Sentence Craft
Other Teaching Tips

Provide a Topic or Foundation Sentence
At the top of recipes you can write a topic or foundation clause students can build upon. A topic might be soccer. A foundation clause might be "The goalie snatched the ball."

Use the Refining Process
At the bottom of the crafting table is the refine area reserved for refining instructions. Here the teacher or student creating a recipe can add specific instructions or expectations. For example, you might ask students to use the extended form of master blocks in the recipe. See pages 104 and 105 for refining ideas.

Use Visuals
Students craft better sentences when they have a visual to inspire them. Display a crafting recipe as well as an image. Have students craft a sentence based upon the image. I first used visuals for crafting sentences after reading Harry Noden's *Image Grammar* and have found success with it ever since. The Internet provides a wealth of image options.

Have Students Create Recipes
Students enjoy creating recipes for themselves or others. See page 22 "How to Create Recipes" for tips.

Make it a Competition
Students in teams have to craft the recipe created by the other team. See page 22 for recipe creation tips. Ensure the principle of no more than two blocks for the middle and top rows is followed. If desired, give students a time limit—no more than 10 minutes. Require students to use extended master block options (phrases rather than individual words).

Use Online Resources
Refer to sentencecraft.blogspot.com for details, including a PowerPoint and random generator.

Write using or inside of the game
See the next two pages for specifics.

Teaching Tips

Teach Using Minecraft.edu

Minecraft.edu is a specially designed version of Minecraft that includes customized teacher tools and blocks enabling instructors to limit or expand what students can do and where they can go. It also allows teachers to create customized assignments.

The creators of Minecraft.edu have made a game that is both affordable and easy to use in classroom computer labs with Macs, PCs, or a combination of both. Explaining the technicalities of how are beyond the scope of this book, but the tech support crew and wiki at Minecraft.edu will ensure you can quickly learn all you need to as a teacher before you use it with your class.

Joe Levin, "the Minecraft teacher," has also made various videos to show examples of classroom use of the game.

I should note here that I am not at all affiliated with Minecraft.edu, nor is *Sentence Craft*. You can teach *Sentence Craft* completely without Minecraft.edu, by limited use of the video game, or by immersing students within it. Below, I will explain ways you can use Minecraft.edu if you choose to do so.

Limited Use of Minecraft.edu

1. If time is limited, or you only have a teacher computer with a projector, you can display the game on the projector as you or one of your passionate Minecraft students, which you'll find in every class from first graders to seniors in high school, demonstrates how to collect wood, craft planks and sticks, create a crafting table, and craft a tool or weapon or two. I find that even this limited exposure to Minecraft helps students better relate to and comprehend the *Sentence Craft* metaphor.

2. If you have more time and/or computers, have students play the game using Minecraft.edu in easy (or survival mode for a little more suspense) and guide them along as they get wood from a tree, craft sticks and planks, build a crafting table, and craft a tool, such as an axe, for themselves.

Sentence Craft

Immersive Use of Minecraft.edu

By immersing students entirely within the game, you can give them writing assignments and provide group activities to reinforce what they have learned from Sentence Craft. Here is an example writing assignment.

Writing a Survival Diary

1. Have students survive a night (or longer) in survival mode and then write a survival diary either in a book in the game or, more practically, in a word processor document after the night is over.
2. As part of the diary, they should briefly explain who they are (creating a character), where they came from, how they got where they are, and what they did to survive (or die if they did not make it). Be sure to require that students do more than simply dig a hole in the ground and wait in it. Instead, they should be creative and resourceful in their survival.
3. Sentence fluency skills: Require that each student use a combination of simple, compound, complex, and compound/complex sentences.
4. Require that students use some of the techniques represented by master blocks in their basic and extended forms: prepositional phrases, participles, appositives, inserted adjectives, and inserted adverbs. Often, as Harry Noden suggests in *Image Grammar*, I require that students underline and label (in parenthesis) an example of each of the above.
5. Peer review. Require that students peer review at least one other students' survival diary, so they can help each other ensure they have used the required techniques and done so effectively. This way the teacher does not need to look for the use of each master technique.

Teaching Tips

Refining Options

The refining option enables a teacher or student recipe writer to provide specific directions outlining the expectations for sentence craters. For example, a teacher may refine a recipe by requiring that all master blocks in a particular recipe be written in series. Below is a list of common refining options at a recipe crafter's disposal.

Simple Sentence Refining Options
SV
- Write a S + V + DO clause pattern
- Write a S + V + Prepositional Phrase clause pattern
- Write a S + LV + C pattern without a "be" verb

SV+
- Write a series of subjects.
- Write a series of verbs.
- Write a series of verbs followed by prepositional phrases
- Write a series of direct objects.
- Write a series of complements
- Write a series of prepositional phrases
- Write a sentence that uses a colon to introduce a series of items.
- Write a sentence that uses a colon to introduce a list of items separated by commas and further organized into sub-categories divided by semi-colons.
- Write a sentence that includes a series of items that is introduced in a way that a colon is not necessary.
- Write a series using conjunctions only, no commas.
- Write a series using commas only, no conjunctions.

Compound Sentence Refining Options
- Use different foundation clause structures for each clause in the compound sentence.
- Write two compound sentences side by side following the same recipe but doubling the batch. You will have four independent clauses and two conjunctions.

Sentence Craft

Complex Sentence Refining Options

Write a short paragraph in which you write one complex sentence following the recipe, and then write at least two more complex sentences with dependent clauses in different locations.

RSV
- Write an essential "who" clause
- Write a non-essential "who" clause
- Write an essential "that" clause
- Write a non-essential "which" clause

Master block Refining Options
- Use basic versions only
- Use extended versions only
- Use a series of three master blocks
- Follow standard punctuation of a master block series
- Write a master block series without using a conjunction
- Write a master block series with conjunctions only

Inserted Adjective
- Use a standard adjective (not a participle)
- Use a past (non "ing") participle

Inserted Adverb
- Use a conjunctive adverb
- Use an "ly" adverb

Use with ½ page journal entries
- Write a ½ page paragraph about __X__. Use the above recipe to craft one of the sentences in your paragraph. Underline the sentence.

Refining Unplugged
- Double batch: write a sentence doubling the recipe.
- Ignore all crafting rules other than including the correct number of each block somewhere in the final sentence.

Appendix

Student Sentence Crafting Activity Sheets
Example Sentences Crafted from Recipe Section
Sources and Other Resources

Sentence Craft Activity Sheet

Name_____ Hour____ Date_____ Score____

Recipe #____ Topic:_____

Practice Sentence:

Your Sentence:

Refine:

Recipe #____ Topic:_____

Practice Sentence:

Your Sentence:

Refine:

Recipe #___ Topic:

Practice Sentence:

Your Sentence:

Refine:

Recipe #___ Topic:

Practice Sentence:

Your Sentence:

Refine:

Practice Sentence Examples

Simple Sentence Keystone Practice Examples (pg. 31)
1: Down the straightaways, around the cures, the Porsche, a European hotrod, skidded and sped down the track.
2: Soaring though the air, the soccer ball sailed beyond the goal.
3: Winding through the reef, the diver, like an eel, squirmed along the bottom of Hanauma Bay, a famous Hawaiian cove.

Simple Sentence Advanced Practice Examples (pg. 32)
4: Blades churning, the windmill swayed in the breeze, rickety and old.
5: President Obama and John F. Kennedy, the thirty-fifth president of the United States, both gave powerful inaugural addresses, their words inspiring the free world.
6: Crippled by an explosion, the Apollo 13, consequently, struggled back to Earth, leaking air into space.

Compound Sentence Keystone Practice Examples (pg. 39)
1: The raft approached the rapid, so we held on tightly.
2: A rooster pheasant crowed outside, so Striker, my Labrador, chased it across the yard, over the fence, and into the field.
3: With a bungee tied to his ankles, Bodee, a daredevil, jumped from my roof, but the knot was too loose, slipping at the last moment.

Compound Sentence Advanced Practice Examples (pg. 40)
4: The caterpillar hatched; the butterfly with yellow and black wings flew away.
5: Dangerous outlaws, Bonnie and Clyde, conceited, greedy, robbed many banks; consequently, officers shot them.
6: Unfortunately, the great oak—its branches strewn across the mountainside—toppled in the storm, and it landed on my cabin, destroying the roof and a window.

Practice Sentence Examples

Complex Sentence Keystone Examples (pg. 48)
1: The lighthouse beamed through the gale as the USS Constitution navigated into port.
2: Santa, because he thought no one was watching, swinging his hips, danced with Mamma beneath the mistletoe.
3: Before the Colorado River, a muddy torrent, flows through the Grand Canyon, it meanders through remote places where Indians once lived.
Complex Sentence Advanced Practice Examples (pg.49)
4: While Tarzan, who lived among the apes, swung through the jungle, Jane waited quietly at camp, her thoughts toward home, her heart aching.
5: Beyond our reach, the sled that my sister had bought me careened down the slope and smashed into my uncle's pickup, ruining an otherwise pleasant evening.
6: Adam, jumping the wake as he twisted and turned, skied into the sunset, while we watched from the boat, while we wondered whether he would ever fall.
Compound/Complex Keystone Examples (pg. 55)
1: Lightening struck the old juniper while we camped on the nearby ridge, but it did not start a fire.
2: Tom, a Hollywood feline, chased Jerry after the mouse stole his food, for they had played this scene a thousand times.
3: Leaping from the foul line, while millions watched, Michael Jordan dunked the basketball, and the game ended in a Chicago Bull victory because of his gutsy performance.
Compound/Complex Advanced Examples (pg. 56)
4: The square dancers, who arrived late that evening, entertained the crowd; Spencer ignored them because his ex-girlfriend was part of the act.
5: The tsunami—overwhelming the flood walls—drowned thousands and decimated the city, but the Tanakas, after the water receded, found their cat still alive, clinging to the roof.
6: Exhausted from the voyage, Captain Sparrow, his legs weakening, headed to his cabin, but he was shocked when he found the door locked and the key missing.

Sources and Other Resources

Killgallon, Don and Jenny. *Paragraphs for High School: A Sentence Combining Approach.* **Portsmouth, New Hampshire: Heinemann, 2012.** An excellent text for introducing and reinforcing sentence crafting activities focused upon incorporating sentences and paragraphs with participial phrases, appositive phrases, and absolutes. This text overflows with professional examples that help inspire students to write like the pros.

Minecraft.edu. A user-friendly, modified version of Minecraft created specifically for the classroom by TeacherGaming.

Noden, Harry. Image Grammar: Using Grammatic Structures to Teach Writing. Portsmouth, NH: Heinemann, 1999. Noden's text inspired me years ago and has been a foundation in my teaching of sentence fluency ever since. Go there to find a plethora of activities using visuals to inspire students to "paint" creative sentences. This book is full of professional examples of participles, appositives, and absolutes.

The OWL at Purdue:
https://owl.english.purdue.edu/owl/
The OWL has, for years, been a flagship website for helping students understand the concepts of grammar and the patterns of punctuation.

Sentencecraft.blogspot.com. Go here for teaching resources related to *Sentence Craft*, including links to an optional PowerPoint and—for teaching in a more dynamic way—a crafting table that generates recipes randomly.

Strong, William. *Sentence Combining: A Composing Book.* **3rd ed. New York: McGraw-Hill, 1984.** This and other texts by sentence-combining-pioneer Bill Strong are replete with "clusters" of short sentences ripe for combining. A typical activity includes eight clusters with four simple sentences per cluster. Students combine the clusters to make longer, more effective sentences. I find that dividing each activity in half (four clusters of four sentences) is effective for a short daily exercise.

Printed in Great Britain
by Amazon.co.uk, Ltd.,
Marston Gate.